BLACK SHROUD
WITH RAINBOW FRINGES

BLACK SHROUD
WITH RAINBOW FRINGES

New Poems 2010-2013

PAUL NEBENZAHL

SILVER BIRCH PRESS
LOS ANGELES, CALIFORNIA

ISBN-13: 978-0615907154

ISBN-10: 0615907156

FIRST EDITION, APRIL 2014

Email: silver@silverbirchpress.com

Web: silverbirchpress.com

Blog: silverbirchpress.wordpress.com

Cover Art: Paul Nebenzahl

Mailing Address:
Silver Birch Press
P.O. Box 29458
Los Angeles, CA 90029

FOR RED

BLACK SHROUD WITH RAINBOW FRINGES

An Introduction

Paul Nebenzahl was the first person to tell me that poetry *didn't have to rhyme*. It was an awakening yet slightly threatening to the world order of language, as I knew it as a twelve-year-old awkward tween. But I got over the shock happily. It was something like the spring during middle school and Paul's sister was my bestest friend. We would create our own hopscotch markers out of broken charms and paper clips and bicycle in the rain until we were lost. And part of our tween expression was writing poetry. Once we read our verse for the family as audience in the Nebenzahl living room. After I read my poem aloud comments and reviews were given, Paul didn't hold back. "It is a *nice* poem but it doesn't have to rhyme." I was taken aback but elated with the freedom.

Paul and I were both raised in Evanston, Illinois, the town of Northwestern University, situated on the Great Lake Michigan just north of Chicago, and at one time living on the same street just blocks away from each other. Part of our common interest was our mutual love of art, music—especially jazz and blues—and, of course, books. We saw each other infrequently after our teenage young adult years, sometimes bumping into each other at the library or meeting at a party. But a reconnection many years later that was intended to be a casual get-together turned into a more meaningful connection for both of us was sparked in part in being able to communicate our recent concerns and insights that we felt we had limited outlets for expressing.

In 2010, Paul visited Europe discovering his long lost relatives who were separated from contact with the devastation of World War II. Alongside the joys of his newfound family he would also learn a darker side of his family history, of cousins murdered, hidden, and those who survived the horrors of the camps. His parents "shielded" him from the truth, yet it was his father who had sponsored a surviving cousin's arrival to America.

Soon after Paul's return from his family reunion in Europe, we met in New York after I had just returned from Austria where I was working on a Holocaust memorial, *Open Heart,* located at the former camp Gusen in memory of Jewish children. Working with survivors, other children, and other publics, I traveled and together we made a memorial out of ceramics. It was an emotional intensity and project that was beyond my limited capacity. With Paul's recent experience I was able to draw upon his reflection to continue the project and move forward. This collection of writing coincided with our forming a relationship with our recent transformative events. Earlier, alone while visiting Gusen and Mauthausen I saw the name Nebenzahl as a named prisoner in the exhibited documents. Being an unusual name I was startled and actually considered informing Paul but decided that I couldn't bring myself to announce then and there that I saw his family name written at the concentration camp as if it was some prize or remains for the day. Later, some months later, we would discover the truth that his cousin Adolf Nebenzahl was indeed murdered at Gusen only a few months before the end of the war.

Unbeknownst to us were these related current events of our personal lives now revealed at our 2010 meeting, I asked Paul to describe how he was processing the information of his newly discovered family. Paul answered with "poetry." He quickly opened his iPhone, and I read two pieces that he had just written—a prose piece and a poem ("Charles Mingus") inspired with meeting his cousin Roby.

Can I even dare imagine that the not-allowed thought is real, a
Keepsake
In my family's twine
That we are connected over blood and time

Roby would join us for the next two years at the annual ceremonies at Gusen and Mauthausen to honor the victims and their cousin Adolf.

Holding the iPhone sitting across from him in an Irish Pub waiting for another friend to join us for a walk on the High Line, I couldn't stop reading his prose and verse and told Paul with insistency that he couldn't stop writing. In these two examples, his writing had an authenticity, a genuine impulse of transcribing beyond the ordinary. The poet, not just as historical recorder—but to create a *historical reorder*. He had to write the poetic phrasing for gathering, witnessing *creatively*. Our connection was centered in the safety of our common language: poetry. But his writing was also about the acknowledgement of bereavement and the prospect of reunification. Paul possessed urgency with composing and connecting to a part of himself that he felt was set aside, made invisible by dominant cultural expectations—forgotten or, worse, abandoned. Part of his writing was a testament to his Jewish identity and Diaspora. A claiming of self and a reclaiming of what was taken. And with the awareness, a holistic approach a shift occurred with his search for new meaning and relationships.

Now in 2014 I am so pleased to be writing the introduction to the first book of poetry of Paul Nebenzahl. His poems are written in sequences of tableaux, interpretative representations that are both public and private histories yet entwined. The collection of poems arises out of a personal transformation and the poetry testifies to the journey made, a memoir. His poetic roadmap works as a guide as we meander through family, trauma, and reflections of politics and human transgressions. Yet his writing assures us through wit, charm, and cleverness that the human spirit prevails amidst the chaos, and creativity is part of that optimism. Nebenzahl cannot comprehend nor understand fully the tribulations of the past yet undertakes the impossible task nevertheless as he imagines a future forward and delights in the small gestures of the collective spirit amongst us.

What is poetry and why does Nebenzahl yearn to make it and for us to read it? His method of elevated language demands a closer reading, a more careful pace of rhythm and sound focusing our attention out of ordinary speak. The poet Nebenzahl is able to choose and control with ambiguity, divinity, and decisiveness—rearranging definition. And that is what I gain with his poems, the nuanced space of transition and temperament. His control of words asserts a voicing and begins the process of rejuvenation through language. Poetry becomes active by the doing, the writing, and the reading. The first stage is his intimate exchange, a commitment to his private practice of writing and then sustained in our reading and taking in through contemplating thoughts and feelings through piecing puzzled words. Poetic activation.

For Nebenzahl, his style contributes to the form through his life as a jazz and blues musician in flute and harmonica. He utilizes improvisation or free style jazz to free style poetry. The use of improvisation with a prompt rebels against the institution of prescribed language; who speaks for and speaks to, who listens and speaks to the spirit within all of us. Part of Nebenzahl's craft is his gift of ease, tenderness, and comfort in words so that when you are meandering through the narrative and scenes you are not spoken down to. He is part narrator, part witness, part trickster with his pranks, quips, bon mots, and double entendres.

Growing up as children together, attending the same schools, walking the same streets, and playing in the same parks offered a sense of comfort and familiarity. It was this safe haven of the past that allowed the adult world of reality from the child's world of idealism and make-believe for us to collide and confide in. For alongside our closeness of location and neighborhood we also witnessed student protest and revolt, civil rights and anti-war rallies. His desire to make a difference for a better world into the present day delivers us a consciousness of what it means to respond.

Through *Black Shroud with Rainbow Fringes* Nebenzahl examines notions of identity, otherness, masculinity, racism, xenophobia, and power. Nebenzahl offers a range of emotions and experiences, the unearthing of loss, encounters of gained perspective, the clandestine legacy of family secrets, and his unpretentious valor of confronting his own demons. Through it all, our poet sings for his supper with clarity and humor. This collection at times is hard hitting giving us the go-ahead to condemn without remorse. Refreshing to be free of forgiveness finally, Nebenzahl is able to feel affection and charity even through history and life's bitter intersections with a whistle and a prayer that is both painful and assertive at the same time. But isn't that what art is all about? Nebenzahl's poetic magnitude lies in its attempt to heal while finally speaking out for what should have been said but wasn't. For many of us the lifetime of waiting for justice never arrives yet the wait changes and passage is handed to move ahead with him. Please read and open your soul to the transformation of what poetry offers at its best.

Karen Finley, May 2014

CONTENTS

BLACK SHROUD
WITH RAINBOW FRINGES

AFFINITY

"Lover Man" as played by Gene Ammons is in my head
As I leave the parking garage
Like being blasted with a gamma ray of Love and Soul
Washed over me like a wave of water
Up from the cold Chicago River
Jug (that's what they called Gene)
Also, "The Boss"

Came out of these cold streets
His father, Albert, a major pianist
Called a "Boogie Woogie" pianist
Like being a "Bach" pianist
Just talking about a period in classical music
Is all, American classical music
Student of Capt. Walter Dyett, at Chicago's DuSable High

He ran with a hard crowd
Von Freeman (Vonski) and Hank Mobley
Clifford Jordan and Pat Patrick
Don't know these names? Look!
Your ears will thank you for the trouble
I'll never forget the stir in the community
When they released Jug from the penitentiary
After doing his second federal bit for heroin
His lifeline to death

In 1969 the album cover "The Boss Is Back"
Showed him coming down the steps from an old airplane
His arms outstretched, telling us "I'm Back"
He was ready to DEAL
That sinuous sound wasn't really even NOTES
It was just pure soul and feeling
Out of tune?
No, redefining pitch to merge intonation with love
More African than American

Jug had some lessons to teach us all
That day at Chicago's North Park Hotel
Thank God it's been preserved, when Jug and Dexter Gordon

Recreated "The Chase" one can hear the whole history of the tenor
Dexter and Jug playing the head-games of Prez, the
Braggadocio of Bean, the explorations of 'Trane, the glass
Beauty of Getz, the mastery of Hawkins, the stunning
Surprise that was Rahassan Roland Kirk
Gene and Dex pushing each other with chorus after chorus of
Fire passion intrigue
Opera quotes, blues riffs, bop fragments, growls
Slurs, slips, tricks, grins, cries and sobs, all there

But, for my short money and long heart, I most treasured
Ballads they fought, that afternoon in grey cold Chicago
Dexter played "Polka Dots and Moonbeams," and Jug responded
"Lover Man" and "I Can't Get Started"
To hear these today is to stop, frozen, on the street, and to
Weep, to think that these great American Artists went to the
Joint because of the pain of their love, their disease

It's heartbreaking, like when they beat Lester Young in the
Army jail, when Coltrane's best friend was killed by the police,
When Billie Holiday had to endure the indignity of incarceration
Black genius was a tough master, and still is
A tough place to be, a rough tear to shed

I just want to tell you, Jug, how much I love you
Especially today, with some perception
No one ever touched your sound
Your soul, one note is all it took to know it was you
There it is
The beauty of your inner sphere being strong all these years hence
"Jungle Strut" we'll remember, we'll never ever forget

It's an old canard
The tenor that was like a signature
They had to play their solos note for note
For the crowds that pressed against the stage
And singers would take those solos and write lyrics
"Moody's Mood for Love" the most famous vocalese

All over the world, from tents to palaces
Those notes played over and over again

Our art form, a precious mix
Of western scales, and show tunes
Of French chords, and jungle beats
All we could think of was the stripes
Really yellow
The kitchen door
The cheap rooming house
The short money
The angry fix

One day it'll all be smoothed out
They'll teach 'Trane along with Sibelius
Maybe they already do
But what I see is a hard road to there
Of beat machines, and silver hairdos
Hot pants and scary lipstick
And Byard Lancaster playing on Michigan Avenue
His horn case filled with nickels and dimes
His tears, and his CDs, all for sale
In a slicker, poorer America

Jug, you could have had a house
On Lake Shore Drive
A modern Stravinsky, plying your art
In halls and concert stages
Not the stink house
The cigarette burns
The turned over collars
Of shiny shirts

But I'll still love you
I'll be that one man crying
Leaving the parking garage
To face the cool Chicago morning
With a face wet with your love
I'll sing your songs
And tell my kids about you
The big man filled with love
The sound never leaving my ears
Never leaving my ears

BABY WOKE UP

Baby woke up
Nightmare
House falling down
Like cards
All around bottles
Filled with flames
World tired out
One more time
At the five-yard line

Reagan was 100
Never liked the Gipper
Lies lies damn lies
They told us
Now we have to hear
This again and over
How Black is White
How Up was Down
How this is better

Finally got it
Laughing through the 80s
Lying through the 90s
Sobs all through the 00s
We're on the other side
Now a slimmer reality
Camels running through
Sullen Cairo streets
Whips in a cop's hand

RuPaul has her/his own
TV show late at night
How to walk the runway
Be a girl/boy
Better than the Charlie Sheen
Show that everyone watches
The women come in and out
Of that Malibu screen door
Used confused tanned slutted-up

What's my daughter to think
Need some Chico around here
A Joan Baez record
Fighting songs from the
Spanish Civil War
Take it above ground
Wear your love like heaven
Before they put plaques on
All the houses Ronny lived in
Out in dusty Illinois

I read about that year his
Dad worked at Marshall Field's
And Ron Reagan lived in Hyde Park
They should have stayed
Would have been better
For the Country
Maybe he wouldn't have
Turned out the nursing homes
Emptied out the SROs
Cashed out the "buck with the
Steak" in the checkout line

Now you can justify
Anything that you can do
By harkening back
To that philistine time
Chico would snarl at the TV
And stir her martini wet
Packed a drink in an olive jar
To take on the train
Her last words about Cheney
"That bastard" she said
And died the next day
Got that right honey

I never lived in the Gold Coast
But I sure worked that street
Those girls toiled so hard
To snare the right horse
The guys eschewed books

For pinky-ring worship
Bought art by the pound
Drank into the night
The lights from cars turning
On Lake Shore Drive
A headache is coming on
Turn out the lights

I knew the Kups and Carl Kroch
Drank wine in Abra's nest
Watched Donahue give way
To Oprah
Artis Gilmore to Michael
When my middle name came up
There was cringing
Had to go clean up to Castlewood
To Studs and Ida to find relief
When I met Manny Kaplan
He was wheeled out for lunch
By his house boy across the street
He teared up talking about my Dad
Said that Irv felt the revolution more
But "we were all revolutionaries"

I don't see it that way
All respect to the President of Sara Lee
But I didn't see you in my backyard
When Dr. DuBois was at our home
Or at the Pentagon when my Dad
Was screaming at a kid from Iowa
The kid must have been 19
National Guard uniform covered
With my Dad's whiskey spittle
Didn't see you in Selma
When my Mom went south that
Summer of hate

She had the summer of hate
And I had the summer of love
Four years apart but what a
Difference those years made

I had grown my hair out
And grown up tall and wild
Had walked with my parents
Now walked alone
Caught up in the music
Left my mitt and bat in the yard
Put it all together
Hit out on the highway
We're left with the remains
The leftovers devoid of real
Hate and real Love
We've got this "Charlie" version
It's all lip gloss and heels
Leather and suede
Lies damn lies
Pukey art
We've got our work cut out for us
If we're going to change one damn thing
Educate someone
Clean up Newark have you seen
That mess?

So I understand
When the bell rings at 3 a.m.
When they start robo-calling you
At 5:30 to close the schools
Because why there's a little ice?
It took 27 inches of snow
To close them here in '67
The shelves of the A&P empty
The cars abandoned on the Drive
Now it happened all over again
Except the stores were stocked
If your card worked you could eat

America trapped in front of her
42-inch screens
Watched Egypt fall apart
No one understood
It was too much to take in
Thank God we could watch

The Packers and the Steelers
That's a battle we could comprehend
So how crazy am I
To think about 1942 and 1945
To help my friend scatter
Some love around the memories of
Genocide?
No wonder you woke up
And thought the drapes were burning
In someone else's house
They are.

BACK ON MAPLE AVENUE

Brandywine parfait, strawberry cartoon
Chocolate rolling papers, puzzle rings
What else is in my jewel box today?
Jimi Hendrix, Ass Id Egg, Tim Buckley
The Seed at Alice's Revisited Under The El
Under the rankling, jangling elevated lines
North of Old Town, rolling out for another day.

Had to walk home in the rain
Lincoln Park, The Gold Coast, to Evanston,
Tired feet and stinging eyes, head down in the wind
Hard nose that last mile, Loyola and then Howard Street
Home through the Jungle, unmolested, one more time
Climbed the tree in back, unlatching the attic window
Slipping back into my father's home, among all saints.

We ran wild and the doors of Chicago stood open in 1968
Phil Schuman and I, we told people on Wells Street
We'd just hitchhiked in from Kansas City and
Needed a Place to Crash the Night
Shown into an apartment on the Polish near West Side
Family hot dog leftovers, TV
We spun tales of our past, or was it Minneapolis?

Once we told a guy we were from
There, and HE was from there, then being from
"Central High" didn't cut it, we knew Nothing
Didn't know a street or a mayor or a dime store
Gave a guy money behind a head shop, we're still waiting
Philip dead, and me alive, we'll never see that
Smoke, forty years gone by.

That summer, when I left for California, and the West,
Crossing the country, my folks hired a private
Eye who went to Old Town looking for us
We were on a train bound for Kansas City that Night
Singing songs, singing folk songs, giddy
That I probably broke my mother's heart.
That I maybe broke my father's spirit.

Sat tight against Big Mama Thornton, I was thirteen
She was telling me how to be, and worrying about me
Although I looked bigger than my age
I poured my heart out, into a ten-hole harmonica
Like a miracle, I was dropped directly onto
Howlin' Wolf and Muddy Waters and Big Walter and Sam Lay
Inside the lion's den I sat, with carnage and pure art as twin taillights.

Dad's prism grew, until it was Oft Blessed.
Wove flowers in a girl's hair, wrote
Poems on paper bags from the A&P. Mom was
Keeper of faded campaigns, of the long lost Cause, of
The canard, the grille, the chagrin, the shrug with
An elemental nod upstream to headier waters
The University people were practicing east of Chicago Avenue.

Still proud of our pipes, our tulips and our
Stiff drinks, our differentiation set us apart
Downwind, in need of a rear exit strategy
Old maps of Evanston reveal its sticky past
Of segregated beaches, and private clubs, of
University quotas, for this kind and that
Of hidden lines of demarcation, not to be crossed.

Yet unspoken, not written into covenants
Not painted by Walter Burt Adams, who had the
Brains to leave people out of his Work
Although there is no finer chronicle of our looking at our
Past, our shared time where there was so precious little to
Surviving, but our picture-book moments are quite worth
Remembering.

The ice skating houses, one in each city
Park, with potbellied stoves and benches to change into
Skates, brought together belly to belly the
Serfs and warriors who divided up the weekly pouch
The skimming's or the killings, the pickings or the slim
Who cooked their hogs in fifty-five gallon drums
On a beach made for croquet, and ice cream chairs
And white gloves, and summer dances where we weren't quite welcome.

The pancake breakfasts, the hobby shops
The bakeries and grocers and beaches, alleys, railroad tracks
We owned it, rakishly sauntering, Whole Territories
Our Own, our Gang Control the Honor of Placing
Flowers on Those who Entered our Domain
When I say we owned it, that's wrong, we owned
Nothing, for we pledged forever poverty, and forever Eternal Love.

BLACK SHROUD WITH RAINBOW FRINGES

Not that many police jobs for artists these days
The chalk artist who very carefully traces the victim
On the street a holdover from Weegee days
The courtroom sketch artist losing ground
To the technology of the court the cameras the smart phones
What's a budding cop artist to do?

That leaves the weekend oil painter
The tree limb collector who strings together
Really lashes those limbs into fashion
But the painter scared of the Gacy clowns
And the sculptor saddened by the demise of the
Automobile bumper and the lack of lashable limbs

So inside my soul my own cop painter
Schooled to document my internal crimes
Those of passion of greed of sad intent
Is hopelessly underemployed
Looking for enforcement work
In all the wrong places

Interior sketches in pencil
Photographed onto my iPad
Taking testimony from my eyes
They have seen the past glory
Of intelligent responses to
Timeworn questions where were you when how etc.

Guess I'll hang my oils out to dry
Behind the old constable bricks
The huffs of wind from criminal cries
Maybe they'll capture the sad tales
Of my crimes of boredom and slack
I sang of older days when pen strokes meant real time served

CHARLES MINGUS

A poem for my cousin Roby Zahler in Antwerp, Belgium

Did we discover "Reincarnation Of A Love Bird" at the same time?
Did we ever imagine that we would share the printed word,
Or strawberries, and wine?

But there you did go, and there I went too.

Can I even dare imagine that the not-allowed thought is real, a
    Keepsake
In my family's twine
That we are connected over blood and time

How I want to storm back in time! How I want to be a blanket
For the Nebenzahls, how I want to rip free the doors and windows
Of Mechelen, and bring everyone home to America
To baseball, and ice cream, and fireflies on summer nights
In our backyard

If what we know of reality is only a child's game of
Chance, then to imagine that the pendulum, for that is what it seems to
Be, has swung back and opened a door to
Another perfect world, where
They
Seem to be
Us

(And not shape-shifting creatures, created in a lab
That Google must have somewhere, our replicant monster
Other selves in creation. A wax nightmare.
Faking our tears, our amazement, our wonder and grief.)

We stared in bewilderment, mutually. We went right to the source
Of our wonderment and stared it down, both of us
Filled with terror and awe.
We stitched together a new narrative, a new story
With gulls, and plugs and sockets, and
Candles of the sweetest odor

Did we know that Dannie Richmond, who didn't really play
Drums
At all, would be a dual backbeat as our heads
Expanded, in 1973, with Jimmy Knepper and Mingus
Trading fours, and shouting at each other,
Propelling a smile—an all knowing, we'll be together
Someday
Smile,
At the corners of your mouth, and mine as well?

It Was At That Moment when an improvisation literally cracks open your
Mind, I looked at the clock.
It was precisely 10:37 pm. On September 4, 1973, and I was
Sitting in my family home
Listening to Mingus. I made a Note to Myself and then spent a
Considerable amount of time
Figuring out where I would be able to find it 40 years hence
When I decided to put it in a jar, and bury it in the backyard
Of our old place in Evanston

The Note must have said
I heard you
Through the needle of my record player
I detected a Sound!

My cousin
Under the ocean
Wanted a mitt like mine, and to fling the ball across the sandy lot
With negro children
And a Green River, cold as ice, and "The Wolfman"
Shown on a bedsheet,
At the Y down the street

And now, he's found
Mingus. He even read the Mingus autobiography
In English, even found Elmo Hope and Grant Green
Lurking around the docks with Toots, and
Henry Miller, and Jean Genet

Bingo!

My father would have filled his pipe, and smiled his impossibly
Handsome smile, and slipped a hand into the pocket of his
Yellow sweater
The lines of fathers, grandfathers, great uncles, old men
Old Nebenzahls
Gathering in the afternoon
Your Dad, and your David, and my David too
A Shabbat where the men are quiet, but easy among themselves
Proving nothing
To no man, nowhere
When Mingus went Crazy, nutso as a loon, and was Locked Up In
Bellevue, his thoughts went Clean as a whistle
That's when he knew that he could peel his skin off, and
Pass for a Jew,
Or an olive-colored Arab, or a Swede

It's why "we" liked jazz, and Mingus in particular. It fit "our"
Conformity
Expressed in my note, under glass, so to speak

And, oh, dateline Antwerp!
You made possibly the same drawings that I was making with
John Nakazawa, of clouds that were also space vehicles,
Disguised as Clouds,
With major retro cool things that only John and I could draw

His dad had interrogated the pilots whom flew the Pearl Harbor
Bombings. His uncles were in the internment camps. That
Was
Big, bigger than the book we had about the
Jews
(We also had one about Negroes, as well, with my mother's leaf press-
ings
In every other page, brittle as dust, Negroes were a big deal.)

I knew someone's uncles and aunts had been dragged to their
Deaths
At the end of a railway line, off a box car, their
Coats
"No Longer Needed"
Their mouths curled in fear

I just never, ever imagined
Even when I was making that note about meeting you 40 years ago
That the people getting off that train were
Our
People
Yours and mine.

Now, I know that. It makes it hard to sleep. Also, when
You
Think hard in the
Morning, and I'm trying to sleep in the America,
It's pretty damn noisy, so pipe it down

My Cousin.

DREAM ANALYSIS

Woke to a dream of crinkled sheets and the corner of my mouth
Wet awake asleep
I dreamed we were walking in Washington, D.C. at
Night dark silent
And you let me slip my hand in yours as we
Drifted without feet
Past armed sentries and Chinese tourists
Suddenly seeing trees
History had known, and maybe made their branches
Low slung wires
Held them together, and aloft, the strangely powerful
Curled smooth skins
Of witness, to war, to famine, depression, anger, despair and
Victory Sweet Jubilation
How did we wind up in a bar filled with silent Black people
All ridiculously drunk
Where I was made warm by the side of a great Doberman's
Gleaming Studded Necklace
And the massive strength of his ribcage pressed against my
Leg warm warmer
I counted three hundred steps from the front door to the
Back again again
And waited for a glimpse of you, a scarf across your face,
Eyes Not Watered
Determined to stand in front of you, and sink to my
Knees Bold Night
And hold you like a tree
Very Very Close
So I could feel your black sheep breath, your public snarl, your
Private Amazing Garden
We found a ladder, and propped it up against a Federal Wall
And Looked Over
Did they just build that? Or, has it always been so? Did those
Broad Expansive Steps
Carry slaves without shoes, or Jews without slaves
Over Any Hump
We seemed capable of traveling, effortlessly, liquid, silent
Private Soundtrack Included
Of chipping away at the brainpan, to reflect memories submerged of

Libraries Poems Blue
The whole thing took place in a box, with an eagle hovering overhead
Looking Looking Looking
You showed me your shoulders. They were clean and strong. You
Told Me Then
About the window you had to climb out of to escape, and of the
People You Carried
In your head, the ones living and the ones
Dead.

DREAMARIUM

This is what kills me
There were dreamers in the transports
Clouds for minds in the death marches
In the last days of the firefight in the ghetto
Some still looked at the ends of their fingers
In awe of the slow turn of magic in mind's eye

See we can't account for the way a shoulder felt
One who strokes their own shoulder
This pulse a key to the engine
The soft machine of reckless imagination
Knowing no bounds and only light beams
The self-contained kind we think think think

Endless every star all knowing
Never seen starker landscapes
From the perch they gave us these dreamers
With pens and talked into recording machines
As we slip the imagination in the dreamarium
Where the sliver of souls still turn 'round each bend

FALL'S ANATOMY

A fall frost
The first, just a sliver of sheen
Of silver on green
Forget that she's swept a pile of
Red, orange-tongued yellow leaves into a
Curious pile, and then the wind took
Them back too

It is said that we're declining now
The year running to empty
Even as markets bustle
The swarm of mankind keen on
Getting the last drop of the
Year to keep, to spend
To stave off

What comes next
Tumult in the lanes
Ice and madness
Old men tearing at their brows
At misguided endings, and
Misplaced dreams that
Cut them quick

But say that fall is the emotional season
And you have spring to deal with
Call fall operatic, maybe that's
Closer still to the center
For lead roles, often the domain
Of the most advanced in
Years remain owned

By fall's friends, the fruit that requires
Baking, the need for a collar
The clearing more open, the tree line
Sparse and quiet
Each morning designed to reflect back
To the writer a clean
Page of plenty

Fall falls back, we return to the classroom
We bake our bread and read our books
The bus ride is longer, but we
Settle, the things in our sack
Prepared for the expanse in time
Between here and there we are
Quiet reading still

And the heart flies back
Led by olfactory, or auditory clues
To remembered, not current
To familial, not adopted
The manufactured detached still
For one who seeks
The Real Deal

But fall is a respite, an in-between
To stop and think is what she
Offers us, the space 'neath the trees
The flowered lane, a little haggard yet
Proud still, with sedum and sage
This year's harvest under a moon
Huge with light

A time to move, to scurry
To cover roots and sew a field, to
Shut off entry at foundations
To the small mammals that are around
Near us, watching us, needing us, needing
Our heat and homes with so
Many blessings aplenty

Soaring mind and vision
Roam the Midwest tonight
A mind's drive to Michigan
Up the old way to camp
You'd pass a million maple trees
Tall and solemn, waving
Strong yellow branches

A pass over the quilt
Down the rivers that matter
The big one that cuts the country in half
The tributaries that shoot upward
On maps where south is down
North is up there
Right on top

Here's what she says to us, this
Dress up spooky time so
Misty and smoky, when one burns the ends
Of corn and hay stalks left in the field:
"Dance with me! Dance on the earth!"
Drink the malt that's been brewing
Letting nature creep

Then hunker down, and study
Layer against the wind
You'll ride out the winter
Chin against the glass
All nature's gifts before you
Even if often just out of reach
Watching snow drift

Keep the fall, its smells and feels
Tucked in a waist pocket close
To take a peek, once or twice
While the snow flies, one might
Colors that flare against the grey
Middle of winter, fall's anatomy
Providing strong medicine

Until the flares of spring
Leap through the earth
Tearing toward the light, the warm
The Promise of nurture
The friendship of water
The elements of success
Winning every year

Keep her close, fall's blanket
Even as you scatter
She'll rake you into a pile
No longer able to use a child
As a tamper to stomp the leaves
Reflection replaces that joy with
Quiet slower days

FAMILY SECRETS

Overture

For what be a family if not a collection of stories
Under which surely lies a collection of secrets
Secrets to save the family soul
To damn it to hell, as well

As we came out into this world
Down leafy Rogers Park lanes
A synagogue on one end, a school on the other
With steep steps between, that's where I plunged

Sorry bloody teeth crash, maybe a neck twist
Cured with an Affy Tapple
Sleeping on my Mom's porch
Like a tiger in the sun, in short pants

My Dad acted as if he came from Mars
But his ancestral home was only three short blocks away
Today I can drive that loop and see both
In two minutes, tops, past low slung kids in Yankees caps

Allegro

We had public secrets to cover the private ones
There were communists in our home
Trade unionists, drunk in our yard
They once gave the bums rush to federal agents, out the front door

But being a Red, marrying one
Hardly qualified as a secret
It was more like a badge of honor, or courage
To face hate with love, with organized passion, with a drink

For an army drank on its brain
This army of city martyrs
Ate, slept and drank sideways on its brain
Laying for all to see, with frequent letters to the editor for further
    identification

Early on my Dad was "tried" and convicted
By a court of fellow Reds
Accused of being a racist, in 1955
He crossed someone's line, and paid a heavy cost

So when the Party split, into China Reds and Russian ones
My Dad went Russia, and enemies were made
Imagine that! A theoretical schism
Among genteel and educated folk in hats and gloves

Now it seems, a scandal created
In an FBI office, where half the memberships
Of Communist America were filled out and mailed in
The whole thing engineered to split and destroy them

Sincere men and women
Idealistic in their ways
Misled, yes, but pure
Their full hearts the only ones in America you could really trust

For they were unfailingly there
When the bodies were cut from the trees
When the workers were shot in their eyes
By Pinkerton's men, who lusted for Red blood

Adagio

The girl from Peru, Illinois, from East Moline
Who could write, and paint and play a modest piano
Who worked in a bookstore in Chicago's Chinatown
Who discovered, at the age of thirty, that she was a hidden Jew

Left home with Bill Coates, married him to get away
A favorite short martini story
Even though the longer version
Was deeper, staggering really, a cauldron of pain and grief

For Bill was sick, and mad with loath
He hated himself for saying no
To his best friend, on a Merchant Marine ship
Parked in the Pacific, waiting for orders

His friend who loved him, and gave his troubled
Closeted gay heart to Bill, on board that vessel
Bill pushed him away, physically, spiritually, emotionally
His friend's body washing against the ship's stern that evening

Back in Chicago, Bill made a list
Of streets he couldn't cross, and trees he couldn't trust
Each list got longer, and as they grew
His sanity shrank, eventually a legal chit for Mom to leave

But they lived at Ritchie Court, in the Gold Coast
Shoulder to shoulder with the hobnobbers
Bathtub gin, and hip flasks
Dark city streets, with flickering filaments

Chico upstairs, holding onto Bill
As he shrank into his clothes like a sci-fi movie trick
And Irv down below, in his crisp uniform
With his Dorothy and her pinup eyes and chin

Dorothy was a flirt, they said
And slept with men at noon
While Dad worked, or looked for work
Or drank his day, with other men, on Milwaukee Avenue

Did he flirt? Was the Pope Catholic?
Did he drink away the day and night
With men who fought and came back home to work
The underdogs, the Reds, the scurvy tide

It all ceased to be attractive, and took on a denser odor
Of oldness, and sadness, and brittle brittle bones, the
Comfort of midnight flesh, in mad positions
In the vestibule of Ritchie Court

Where they met, my Mom and Dad
Their own marriages in shambles around them
Mad about each other, they smothered the hurt
With the cool touch of skin, standing in the humid night

Vivace

Did they bay at the moon, at bankers and trusts
Because they didn't have their own? I think not.
I never questioned, even today,
That the fight was real, based in ethics, tried over time

The call of working people
Combined with the plight of the poor, the Blacks and Mexicans
Buried near the highway, away from the grotto
In a racist South Side cemetery, that was the drumbeat they urgently heard

But life is mundane, and only a collection
Of mornings that sing, and those that sob
A private eye, with a camera and a flash
Kicked down that hotel room door, Dorothy's bottom bare in flight

The same Dorothy whose glamour shot
Stayed in our family pictures
Long after she moved to the coast
And acquired a pool boy, a driver, and a Rolls

My concern here, in peeling back this onion
Is not to revel in the victories of my parents' defeats
For they lost, true and simple
Look at the world today

My calling is more pronounced and more painful
For seeing under the hem, the skirt, the robe
Revealing the lumps, the scabs, the scars
Of simple people, who fought long and hard, and meant so well

By the time I came into the picture one quarter of the secrets had been
    buried
The original sin of my parents' union
Underneath it all, pulsing daily
Driving us, in Ramblers and Lincolns, taking out the trash

When I discovered that the Rosenbergs were guilty
Not innocent! Not vanquished.
Then it all came into question
The cruelty losing whatever slim justification that false history provides

Then the *Free Morton Sobell* dinners with the loud people
All over my house, the coats piled on my bed
The middle-aged couple, overcome with altruism and booze
Under the coats, laughing, mixing their old juices together

Allegro (reprise)

I never thought it was an even fight
When my Dad kicked my ass
When he hit David over the head with a gallon of milk
And David ran back in the room, throwing his penny collection
     against the wall

It never looked like it would turn out well
When they started drinking, which was every night
My Dad trying to ride my bike in the hallway, dead drunk
His once gay laugh a death snarl of fright and fear

They should have busted him for a DWI
That night he was hunting my sister down
I saw her head hit the door of his car, at Clark Street Beach
Like a ragdoll, it bounced, and he stuffed her into the back seat like a pro

David had it the worse, hands down
Driven down Ridge Avenue, in an ambulance
Going back to the P & P locked ward, in a straightjacket
Right by our big, suburban house

Before they gave him the drugs, the gag
Before Freaky Jerry tried to poison him after he talked to the cops
Before he was surrounded and pummeled by ten thugs on an Oakland
     Street
This was all prelude to that

Never learned how to fight, just to run
Holding his violin case, not much to protect himself with
They beat him every day
Took his lunch money, his wallet, and left him colorless and pale

"Be A Man," my Dad would bellow
And deliver a new blow, the one that hurt the most

Observed by siblings, who had to watch
When an ass-kicking was ordered and delivered

It's a step away, just a step
From beating your kids to beating your wife
The screaming nights, the neighbors see
Lights on and off, doors slammed right off their hinges

My Mother on the couch, never been like this before
She didn't know what house she was in
In Moline, or with Bill, or my Dad
She thought a tree limb had knocked her out cold

See this, and running upstairs
Not knowing where to go, or hide
He was coming up, and he was mad
My ass was grassed

For who was I to hit in return? I was leaning toward Love as a profession
If the ministry were available I might have taken it
How can you work for peace and justice
And then beat your own children into a pulp?

Adagio Con Alma

My sister and I were downtown one day, in the Loop
Entering the subway, down the stairs into the cool and the dark
My Father walked past us, coming up the stairs
A woman on his arm, he was smiling and deep in quiet conversation

We shrank into the shadows, as if on cue
Wordless, knowing our jobs, we followed them
Into the Pittsfield building, where the elevator they entered
Could be monitored on a bank of screens against the wall

Sitting in the coffee shop, hidden by the Chicago *Daily News*
Looking at the lobby, to see him returning
The building's doorman, ever helpful
Pointing out the nervous children

"What A Surprise!" A big Irving show
The woman, Oh! we just ran into each other

So the lie started, one we followed, my sister and I
With startling attention, and passion, and detail

We learned her name, we told our Mother
We called her husband, a doctor, on the phone
We followed him, at night, down Main Street
One-armed, in shirtsleeves, at the pay phone across from the A & P

Lisa was blindfolded and taken in his car
One-armed, he favored Mercury Lincolns
A basement apartment, somewhere in Chicago
Where he removed the blindfold and ate Chinese out of cartons

I never saw the place, but visited hers
Her sixteen-year-old apartment, across from Robert Crown
My Dad paying the rent, a boyfriend moved in
My Mother, now mad, alone in a 27-room house

We all lived somewhere else. I lived with Mark
We lived on the beach in Rogers Park
I played an angry flute solo into the telephone
And hung up on her, drunk in her despair

When Mark married Martha, before she lived and died
She told me that her Father was admitted to the Fourth Floor at
    Evanston Hospital
The crazy floor, I remembered, from when I worked there
My Mother was with Peter Senn on that floor

Where was I? I never knew that she was hospitalized in that way
David at Michael Reese, Chico on Evanston's Fourth Floor
My Father mad in his own way, but controlling the strings
That ran the family's way, our beingness, our everything

Maybe that explains what happened when she was dying
I kept bringing her back to the ER
Or the paramedics who had to take her out of her refrigerator
Where she was stuck, and put out a smoke in the butter dish before
    being rescued

The nurses would cluck, they would scratch
And the clock of medicine went backwards, or sideways
But never forward, never better, never hopeful
Her dying like sand through my fingers, no matter how hard I tried

They didn't say it, but there was the air of
Caring for damaged goods
The secrets of her chart, we never saw, even when we asked for every page
After I collected her wedding ring from a man in a dark room under
    the hospital

FLY OR DIE

It took a long time to get to even order the wings
Can you imagine waiting for your wing order
And being on the telephone with someone in Bangalore?
Modern times never looked so rough

Understand then waiting your whole life to even make your order
And when you get them, a big boot steps on your wing
It's a multi-colored rainbow monarch splashy wing
Now it's crushed under a hard nasty heel

Fly or die it said on the fortune cookie
Time to fly the trees whispered to me
On my childhood street
Old haunted trees giving me strength to launch

I found my own strength that's the only way
One can fly
Buttressed by my own fuel and oil savings
Jettisoning cargo to keep afloat the smile rises

Up over the streets that said one way
From up here you can see their two-way past
Up over the canyons of youth and casualness
The callow crag of early juice no reason

Soaring now scary as shit
For the linear is blurred by the burn of atmosphere
The earth a lisping blob of stuck-together dirt
Whirling through the dark night like a shuddering fish

Encircled by a billion lights
I'm flying round the orb in looping traces
My wings flash over the cool green waters
I chase my flying soul over crest and wave

Finally looking the little card in my pocket
Taking it out at blinding speeds
I can make out the handwriting
"Calmer" the note said

There's an answer
Calmer and stronger still
These waters will make my nights quiet
Wings wet from the river now drying

In the light my lord my love
In the light of a good person I was taken
In the gaze of mysterious deity
Hard urgent hands fast on the helm

Hand on mine eyes on mine
Wings stronger still for the journey
When they tear and rip and fail then
I'll already be there, again, already there

FOREVER MIDNIGHT

To be forever midnight
Is not necessarily to be forever blue
For midnight comes with its own box of hues
Some blue, to be sure, and some
Gossamer and sheer as first mist
While other midnights are all lit up
(for we are always pressed nose against the glass)
Throngs stream through when you're
Always a little blue
Horns and stomping feet
You shrug, the nonchalant
You know to do, and hard collar the corner

To be always noon
Always waiting on the platform for the 12:05
Sun streams through your eyes most days
Books, and gloom, and funk
Not often partners are they with noon
(for we read in the morning, we fret at night)
The list endless of people who tug your sleeve
Passing the midday hour in transit
Holding a table
Catching your breath at the corner of an old
Downtown where quiet streets slant over shade
Looking up a window shifts its glare

Like thread my children move
They have needles on their hands to sew their way
They wrap me up, from different sides
They employ the Trojan Horse
The Hallelujah or the Hail Mary
Always winning while I'm always receding
(for we are cruel or just as parents nothing more or less)
They rule the night that intersects my arc
My cool and always midnight mark
Long after I'm lost in a stanza or a caprice
They're mix mastering it all into
Their own flat message slipped into a waiting open pocket

FUNERARY DAY

Today you say goodbye to a friend, who left this world with a last
Whisper that included your name, who placed in your hand a
Drawing of life itself, and quietly slipped away. It is in
Honor of this life, beautiful still, that this poem comes, as we
Wonder at the mystery and the majesty of our life force, and
Grapple with its fall and winter seasons, and the end when
Snow covers the land and blackbirds beat a path across the sky.

Look, at what we see:

In many cultures on this human earth the dead still live in the family,
     in the
House, in the heart, their presence a part of daily life
The dead do the dying things and the family the living ones
And together they face life with the cold stillness of death at the door
The seaward motion of the clocks on the wall
Listing toward home, toward solace, toward resolve, ever onward.

Think then, about this:

On the cold Midwestern plains the Arapahoe huddled, driven from the
Rainmaking lands that their great Mother gave them, and that they
In turn stewarded in Her Honor, their bison skins stretched in the
Sun and their fires stoked. Here they collect their dead for a
Great Sun Dance, and they tell the stories of the dead to keep the
Memories fresh. Great warriors and root collectors lay together,
Strong noses pointed skyward on the cold winter ground,
Yet they are disconnected from their trees and the spirits that live
Within. This disconnection affects their sleep, their speech, their
Power, their inner light. They are fading like a dying battery in the street.

Take out the Death Snapshot. It might look like:

From a hot church, under black umbrellas, comes the band, trumpet,
     drums,
Trombones. The march to the church was slow and steady, the drums
Roll, the trumpets mourn. We are laying the brother down, we are
Putting him in God's hands. Now the pace quickens, the sweat riles,
Call and response driving simple blues notes upward as roll call for the

Day, the remembrance of the brother a community dance and sweet
Prayer. We bury our dead above ground, and when the levees burst,
Corpses float in the streets, and God weeps her yearly tears when
Words and deeds fail us, reverse us, confound us and confuse us.

And yet a terrible story is on everyone's lips:

A child goes into the water. He slipped into the black brine to wash his
Feet, but he was only ten and the current knew his every move. The
    father, a
Cambodian man who fled the Khmer to find poverty in Chicago,
    returns to the park each Day where It happened.
He knew, we all knew that there would be a day when
Police would push the reporters away, when the slack-jawed man would
Bellow and writhe on the ground. When we would cease to
Understand our world, our cruel God, our uneven rulers. For we do not
Live lightly in the land of death, no, we live a heavy life where
Death does not comfort, does not take us home on sailing ships led by
Sirens calling our names, does not wash our bodies and place them
Gently alongside those of our Mothers.

We examine our own patterns of behavior:

We start to read the obituaries at a certain vintage, we scan for names we
Know, or ages close to ours, the crosses and stars of David and
Old photos catch the newsprint and hold its black sheen.
Each time a death bell goes off, we gasp that it has happened again!
But we know, each of us and all of us, that so it ends as it began, in
Mystery, blood and wonder, on a fine afternoon in a flowered field, or a
Quiet room, the dank green walls recording another passing of time and of
Person. We eat, sleep, walk and work, read and think, swim and cook,
But we do not die. We have death heaped upon us, just when we can't
Think of another thing that can happen, just as we've figured it all
Out.

A collector's song:

Pyres, caskets, prayers, Styx. The currency of our death is a dark
Image of this world, and some who Live feast on its images and its
Vibe, so strong that it invites Life to live dead while alive.
We are grateful dead, we die the little death, it's "killing" when it's

50

So good, "You're killing me" when funny, Wisconsin death trip, "You
   slay me."
We wear skeleton T-shirts, Day of the Dead masks, sleep in caskets, our
   movies and
Books about drinking and draining blood, an endless supply of
   celluloid blood we
Manufacture and distribute each and every day...

And, an attempt at reason:

Yet there is no fear like eternal fear, no better marketing scheme for
Popes and shaman of all callings, no hotter mystery, no better
Bookseller's competition. The world stops for death, but only
Lady Di really stopped us cold in our tracks, "Not her!" the
Rabble cried, and each city hosted a flowering, bejeweled shrine. We
became a World Religion of Diana's Death. We breathed as one. It
was more dangerous than a billion Chinese jumping off their desks at
the same instant. The controllers at the controls had To Stop It All;
when the whole world stopped breathing, and then exhaled together,
to
Keep the axis from spinning out of control, the world became a
   pinwheel blown asunder
And teetered toward disaster, toward chaos, toward infinity, ever
   outward.

A gathering of lists, that come from Tribes:

Death's final instructions sound like this
Leave me on an ice floe, Leave me on a mountaintop, Commit me
   to sea
Bury me under the earth, Lay me under a tree, Mummify me
Keep my jaw in a jar, in a sanctuary, Burn me up and scatter me
Chop me up and repurpose me
Remember me, Read my poems, Sing my songs, Tell my stories
Stop to think of me
Name a living thing for me, a child, a tree, a star
A shining, shining sea

A Prayer for sanity:

Mostly we tell God

Remember me, please, remember me

My Prayer:

And, so now I pray
Make a new civilization in my name, my image, using my bones and my
Ideas for building blocks
Study my twitches, my gasps and groans
Wonder at the living I did, when it was my time to Dance!
Weigh my breath, my blood, my air, my thoughts
Catalogue what I have left behind, for we like lists.
And, then
Let's learn something that we can
Use,
For the next time around.

GOD IS GREAT

Skin and Flesh and Teeth and Bone
My family gave all, then died alone
Pushed off trains, lined left or right
Left for slavery, right for death that night

A scar a thousand miles wide
Was left on our family's soul, our pride
Our knowledge of our roots or place
Our verve, our stature, our need for grace

Was something different about our kind?
Growing up, some did opine
While the jackboot never came this way
Its cruel sting was felt each day

The numbers on a neighbor's arm
In Rogers Park, did cause alarm
Then we moved across the border
Where 7,000 in Skokie were scarred by horror

To find my faith? So easy to drift
But choices, unclear, are difficult to sift
We need our religion, and then not so much
We easily wander, in and out of touch

Until something tears at our chest
We react, we right our selves, at best
The searchlight flickers on and off
We look for clues, and find the cloth

The holy books, the looks so stern
The hard-backed seats, the incense burn
A group in prayer or wracked in grief
Time is a blessing and also a thief

The year is marked with pious thought
As ritual soothes, its benefit bought
Through labor, genius, gestures of love
And questions of the efficacy above

Our Lord is cruel and often blind
To suffering humans and blundering mankind
But unerringly sweet and unfailingly so
To wrens, and robins, trapped in the snow

A priest, a rabbi, a saint, a sinner
The connection does each generation grow thinner
To connect these dots, and find the path alone
Is much to ask, from the street to the throne

For our flesh and our minds are slaves to the times
To fashion, so bold, to unleash tongues of mimes
To temptation, to action, to confession, to redemption
The human condition a test of resolve to submission

When we fail, when we fall, when we lose peace of mind
When our faith is tested and our tempers unwind
When God is a mystery not to be found
When music is a mechanical, tedious sound

Look between the obvious clues
Listen to teachings of Hindus and Jews
Of Sufi who suffered and Baptists unglued
Whose Pentecostal uttering border on rude

Find the peace that is offered, even if odd
Is the pitch that accompanies the words or the rod
That strikes fear into us, and drives us on down
To a supine position with our eyes to the ground

For the mystery of God and Her minions is vast
We never see the whole screen moving so fast
But the curve, the shape, the gesture in flight
Gives pause to the possibility of Right

Of order, and justice, not chaos and muddle
Of purpose, and method , not a trap or a puddle
We Hope, I do, although hope is a friend
To only those with a predetermined end

For we know, remember, and remind ourselves so
That this cruel God let our people go
The basket in the river, babe eaten by snakes
The innocent children all victims of rakes

Then God pulled the switch, or She turned away
As Ruth got off the train that day
The hand said *right*, and she stumbled there
The sunlight shone in her flaxen hair.

GUSEN STATION

Tumbled torn asunder
Tied-in, light and air choked off
The odds of light shafts through slats
Diminished by the rest of the travel
Light would have to make through
Holes in cloth, already broken
Emaciated, really
Stacked like baggage from the farm
But loaded in a fancy train station
Maybe at night, and maybe not
Everyone was already looking the
Other way, so few if any saw
No one not one of them noticed
Two cattle cars filled with sacks
Moving like they were alive
But they were already dead
God had taken their souls
In the middle of the journey
And gathered them up, crushed
Like a chestnut wafer
Offered at communion
The cars quiet as they rolled
Through brilliant scenery
Inside there was no more
Time to think or to soothe
Broken wrists and bloody ears
So the train rolled through the
Evil dark night
In the morning the bags were
Pitched onto carts, and
Pulled to the camp
It is said that a woman was
Going to have a tooth pulled
And she looked sideways
As the sacks were lifted and thrown
One by one, stacked on long
Pushcarts, and pulled by porters
Here and there a whimper or
A scream muffled by cloth

Seemed to come from the pulsing
Mass of burlap, but in the end
All was quiet in alpine paradise
Not a crumb out of place

HE HURT YOU BETTER

I thought abstract poetry
Was the dominion of and at the command of President John Fitzgerald
    Kennedy
And the dictum of Oscar Wilde, and John Lennon,
Susan Sontag, and Yoko Ono,
Harry Belafonte and Judy Garland,
Goldie Hawn, Artie Johnson, and the Gabor sisters

That's where we lived
Every night these people crawled into the home
You began to expect that
Paul Lynde
Would walk out of your loo

That Professor Irwin Corey
Might be ironing a shirt in your kitchen
Watching Walter Cronkite and the evening news

You'd be there
Stuck with Don Rickles
Yelling at you, at the same time your family was
But all so much better he yelled he hurt you
So much better than them

HERE'S TO THE SINGER OF SONGS

Here's to the singer of songs
The siren of adventure
Who crept into my chest cavity a few nights ago
When it was hot, ghastly so, and the teepee room
Dripped with its own cedar sweat

For I was thinking of tearing at my skin
When I had shed my clothes
The cool bath hardly helped
I paced nude from back to front
Looking for a break in the weather

The dogs, as well, mesmerized by the heat
Laid on cool wood floors and sped up their breath
To cool their pulses, I had half a mind to shave them
Their regal coats it has been explained to me
Served to keep them at an even keel in all types of climes

Thinking about my Mother, who had come from Peru, Illinois
And had grown up in hot, dusty Moline
Her stories of her first year in Chicago
A bohemian summer where poets and their drinking readers
Slept on Fullerton Beach, on fire escapes and rooftops

And remembering my Dad, his early jungle flesh
Was the wonder of Senn High, a gay tenor
He too had talked about things he did
To stay cool when the miles of pavement were burning
Holding the hot sun long after it had passed the coast out west

I was in a tizzy
I imagined the grim reaper was just outside the door
With a hot poker to stick into me again and again
My reading in the bath had been leaning to the thirties
And the forties when men and women burned dead or alive in ovens

You might say I was off the program that night
My darling tucked in seven states away too late to call
The one air device I hooked up to the window and the outlet

Hardly made a dent in the blast
So intense was the furnace that stayed burning long after sunset
Relief, which will often come from the horn of Miles Davis
I play Miles into the night some evenings seeking solace
His long lines stretching out like lanterns on the water
Being pushed by a gentle breeze
His sense of strategy a balm for worry and an open door of wonder

But that night Miles didn't click
Nor did Coleman Hawkins, or Muddy Waters
My old standby saints of sound
Heard them crooked not straight
And put away, finally, the sounds that often calm

Same with television, it made the room hotter
The storylines hard to follow
What was I in the mood for?
Mystery, drama, romance
Closed the computer screen down, and ran ice along my face

Sonny heard it first
A crack of thunder split the sky at two o'clock a.m.
And then the heavens simply opened up
I was transported back to earlier summer nights
When we ran in the rain in the nude in our big backyard

And then both dogs were howling
The thunder chasing lightning, just seconds apart
We could see the street bright as day, brighter
When the lightning struck down the block
And the rain pounded on the roof over our heads

Quiet like, without discussion
The kind that a man sometimes has with his dogs
We lit down the back stairs to see the night storm
And feel the air to find out its nature, we knew
Going down or going up, it was just going

Without a leash we opened the fence gate, and walked to the street
Dogs and I, we let the cool rain soak us
Soon drenched with cool water, hair matted and clothes soaked

The dogs walked right next to me, without a sound
Without a command needed to keep them close

We walked for a hour, the power now snapped out
The whole neighborhood dark as coal
One house at Ashland and Wilder had candles in the window
I could hear the last drinks being poured at the rain party
Inside that hot little house on the corner

I was laughing, low and deep
A belly laugh from way inside
At the turn of events and the pounding rain
It must have dropped thirty degrees
From one hundred to seventy in five minutes flat

My dogs on either side of me
Understanding that this needed to be
They trudged along touching my wet legs
And looking up at me
I swear they were both smiling in the pouring rain.

HOSTA

My garden ringed with hosta
A shade paradise
The plant, from Japan
Like Impressionism, an import
Like the gingko, a transplant
But, unlike either,
A resilient force that defies destruction
Neither snail, not deer, nor human feet
Can really kill the strong shade plant
For next year it will reappear
Fill out its border responsibilities
Keeping these plants in and those out
Ringing the impatiens, weak sisters
That need annual implantation to
Strut their colors
There are perhaps fifty varieties
Sturdy hostas all
Could feed a man
Lost in the woods, escaped from avarice
They could provide the nourishment
Needed to stay alive
But most grow unheralded
Second stringers to the daylily
The rose and iris
That capture the eye's lens
We scurry through the hosta line
In search of a lost ball, or
Running from some trouble
We seek shade from tall trees
But under each hosta
A world unique and moist
Cool and untouched
Suitable for little lives
Remains unmolested

Instant Message

Forms and Ways

Back in the day, smoke was collected
And kept in blankets, and then released
Timed to the chant and beat of a drum
Messages rose over the hills and drifted out

Across the seas, where in stone turrets
Great printing presses were at ready
A new bible was born that evening, and
Pressed for libraries across the kingdoms

In agrarian times to communicate was to *think*
A thought a powerful electrical charge
That leapt from the brow
Telling those connected a story of thought, muted by action

A love letter, closed by wax and sealed tight
Delivered by mail sack on speeding hoof
To the battle brewing across the Potomac
Down Arlington way, now controlled by empire

Farther from home the iron was forged
Shipped down the *James*, and loaded on mules
A thousand black men, there was no limit
To the number of backs broken by going West

And what followed was the clatter, the tick tick
Of white men whose eyeshades covered for shame, as
They clicked the news bad and good up the Ohio and Illinois
And kept a keen eye for the afternoon train

Innovation

Imagine the shock, the nerves drowned by tears
To touch a face and arm, and deliver a thought
Yet in old Chicago, they learned inclusion
Of those whose rapture was visible from down the street

And writers with pens, and old manual ribbons
That needed oil, and ink, and whiskey and beer
Who banged out the headlines, and talked as they wrote
About tomorrow's *trifecta* at the nearby racetrack

Picture Genet with his pencil stub, writing on rolls of waste paper
Wrapping it round his body each night
The flowers unfolding as he told his story
So that others might stave off a similar fate

And Mishima ordering a round of hot sake
To rub on his belly before plunging a knife
Through his gullet, tearing a semi-circle
To ensure his passage to the old warrior's home

Now that's communication
That's remarkable, using your body as a pen
Writing your noble history in blood
That washes away personal sin and delivers salvation

Retrenchment

A huge billboard is going up, right where the
Tunnel takes you into New Jersey
It'll blow smoke rings across the eight lanes
To remind you to smoke that night

Jingles written like lead bullets
To pierce the skull with planted song
That rattle around the cranium
Directing zombie-like our purchases of wares

The airwaves filled with messages
Flying back and forth
The sifting harder now, the blizzard
Taking all of our resources just to think for a minute

A thousand journals stuck between mattress and box springs
Or crammed up on a shelf, up high
The words a journey of emotional shock and awe
Forgotten, like too-small p.j.'s and fuzzy slippers

Language can be code, too
Or dressed up like a walk in the park
But when one arrives in the dead center where directed, is
The field empty, have the crowds dispersed, their echoes silent?

Dear Landlord

Then the little pieces of paper with lists
And notes to remind, and catalogue, and plead
To please come home with the chicken soup
And don't forget the quart of milk

They swirl around my feet each day
As I walk to get my morning brew
If ordered, and numbered, and lined up some way
They'd tell a story of nation in motion

Of people assaulted by words, a tower of Babel
Funny, even as newspapers and books retreat, they're
Replaced by lithium screens of gray black and white
Everyone able to take a book from the heavens for $8.99

Walking, each step in fours, and no cracks to bend
And songs in my head from the oldies station, still on
No whistles, but strides that quickly deliver
My driven procession of leather on stone

I think of the billions and billions of letters
Numbers and words and phrases and quotes
With attached images, and sounds, and links to consider
All thrown in a super collector of symbols

On the El last week, traveling to the Loop
Each face was posed in front of a rectangular screen
Fingers poised to instantly answer
The slightest sign of life from within the thing

I counted 27 iPhones and Droids
At $500 a pop, that's $13,500
A fortune of magnificent proportions
To the haggard man next to me

Who maybe barely made it
To this day, from where ever he started
To sit, and be surrounded by young kids
On a public train, each hunched over a little computer

Maybe it was watching "The Office"
Over a guy's shoulder at O'Hare
When I realized that we were all crazy
I felt sick in a really old way

Payday

Here's to the stone chisel
Here's to the cave paintings of animal and human
Here's to the drums that beat into the night
Here's to the running messenger, pausing at a mountain stream

Here's a backwards salute to the writer, Pynchon
Who wrote out V in longhand
At one thousand pages it qualifies
For a long vacation or a prop for a very short table leg

For a work of that magnitude
Can no longer be expected
The 500+ pages of Twain being released one hundred years later
Affirmation of the paucity of long thought

So gather around my writers
And cast your words down
Find a chisel and a mountainside
And bear down, writing with brawn for time

For it is you who bears witness
Keeps the light of knowledge lit and warm
Who tells us that our stories
Have currency, and might, and right

For what can be preserved? What can be maintained
With provenance for future's past
The whole of human knowledge, expression
Distilled into three short books of truth

You'll want to have a copy of each
And then cast away the rest
We're the know-nothings of tomorrow
Taking tradition off our kitchen tables

For good things come in thirds
Trees, birds, and symphony movements
Stanzas of love, and treatises of hate
All the same, by weight, the heaviness of the words

For the only connection between good and evil
Between love and hate
Between what I save and what I toss
Are the words that stay, long after the close of evening's door.

LILY OF THE VALLEY

Shoshana my people called the early rose, sometimes the *Lily of the Valley*, or
Mary's Tears, wept at the crucifixion, or when Eve was torn from the
  Garden
These many names of the first spring flower that my Mother used to
  collect
On that day when the earth seemed to turn from harsh to soft
That first day was always an event in our house, when the flowers
Small and fragrant, with their shyly down-turned bells
Were gathered and placed in small blue glass jars saved through the
  winter months
We knew then that the ground, still hardened from the final frost,
  would be alive
Soon crawling with insects, and overrun with tulips, and crocus and
  heather
Spring jumpers, they are impatient to leave the earth
To rise out into the early sun, and bask in its short warmth
Between cool nights and short days they bloom and wander in the garden
What an act of faith! Of courage, to burst so when others sleep
Their adventurous nature a signal to those who'd rather not hold back
But risk all to parade their love into the still damp mornings, when
  dew can freeze
Can kill the lot of them, every forty or fifty years, when Nature has a fit
And calls back her shock troops, white as snow, yellow as sun, pink as
  the inside of
A young calf's mouth, seeking warm milk in wonderment as its young
  legs stand

Along Wilder Street, with its wood frame farmhouses and small parish
  church
Where Mary watches, her gilded eyelashes just fresh from the last
  snowfall

The trees are planted in straight lines like farmers used to cultivate
To mark their fields, and remind their flocks
To stay put for feeding, for grazing and for slaughter
Among the homes, still belching smoke from their brick chimneys
The smells of early dinners, and wood fires, and coal bins
Coat the morning air. One can see the even rows of tulips, planted at
  summer's end

Lining the lanes where hoof and wheel once rolled, before rubber wheels
Ran crazy circles around the small blocks of this town within a town
The flowers planted, in the hopes of the start of a season that no one cared for
But all made ready for, in root cellars, in gathering wood and kindling
In slower walks to town to fill baskets with flour, and honey, and lard
For the cold months ahead. Oh look among these orderly rows of spring flowers
So strong for so short a time, but so colorful with their Easter hues, and their
Black stamen—for among them, connected by miles of underground rope
Grow these Lilies, which wander at will, going where the ground might be soft
Enough to let them rise up, a wonderful miracle of prayer and hope

As the young saint in training must watch the lotus blossom rise, its opening
Undetected to the normal human eye, and observe each second of its `flowering
So might we sit on Wilder Street, when the ground is still cold to the touch
When birds stay in the tree line, only swooping down for food when certain
That success will follow risk, or else they must sit and stay
Watching for others to lead and then follow, to finally romp through the skies
In delight, seeking mates to tease and to settle with, to build nests and nurture
Young, watching and waiting for others to lead into the easy months ahead
For we are the risk-takers, the first responders
Who take our paint, our pens and brushes, and put silver flutes to our lips
And signal to others that it is time! Time to come out of our homes
To rise up out of the ground
To shake off the last bit of frost and welcome the Sun
In all of her majesty and early glory
Knowing, all along, that we might fall, or falter
That others might look on not in wonder, but in disdain
At the tight-wire act that our early and pure love signifies

Is it better to wait by the fire, staying safe and stolid
Letting others go first? Then to follow, knowing that the pathways
Will be warm, and filled with beauty, and only needing our trowels
For weeds that have followed the first flowers of Spring?
I think not, for I have seen the beauty
Of the first morning when the Lilies burst forth
Honoring my Mother, saluting the Sun, and carrying Mary's
Tears and her majesty into the easy months from the hard ones
It takes a certain leap of faith to say, "I know," to hear that new
Rhythm of song that only early Spring can sing
To find the right key, right away, not fumbling through all twelve
In this knowing, we lead the others, they stare in amazement
Through frosty glass and across still wet fields
"There they go again!" the cry comes up, and the little town stirs
Now they can go out, now to worry less about warmth and start
Thinking about the journeys, the picnics, the backyard parties
In the easy months, made possible by Mary's Tears, by Shoshana's
White roses, with their bells of perfume, their precious stalks
They will follow precisely because we will lead
And when they finally dance, and string lights against the warm, starry
Nights, we will be gone, turned under, waiting for the cold to make our
Spring plans to love again.

LISTENING TO GLENN GOULD

Listening to Glenn Gould play the solo piano works of
Arnold Schoenberg even with the crackle of vinyl
It is clear that his Bach and Schoenberg are connected
Through a maze of backdoor channels although
Arnold scares and Johann exceeds
A fist full of keys giving way to
Yellow flowers and sour plastic skins
And then the relief! Of the channels Gould chases the
Father to seventeen down lonely and perfect streets
Lanes really he runs the walls of Prussia high, high
The King's mighty army pauses for tea and
Blackberry jam so one little Bach can play the
Leipzig blues in my mind they close their eyes
And when they resume seeing Bill Basie is at the piano
Wearing his sailor's cap and a double-breasted suit
Yes, this I would like to see the powder wigs get they
Mind blown by the few notes he propelled into space

Observing the album cover with Gould posed next to
The iconic Steinway at Columbia Studios on 30th Street
New York City he has on a dark suit and thin tie
The beads of sweat under the brow
The hand on the chair like it was a football
Or a pistol one can almost see the tension
Of the photo shoot in his pushed down wrist and
Biting inside the mouth
Glenn liked Basie and Duke but favored the New Orleans
Players he would go there famously with black leather
Gloves on and not shake your hand

The Goldberg Variations came up in the Steve Jobs book
That appeared one second after his death
That Jobs would listen and compare the two Gould records
The one that launched, and the one that closed, his career
And marvel at the differences in thought and sound
Everyone who owns Glenn Gould as personal
Musical chef and top game-changer dog will instantly get this
The quest for purity
The damned singing and grunting

The left hand from hell
Crispin Glover could play Glenn and play Bill Evans
Without even thinking of the consequences

LOVELY RITA

Split a flower in two
Perfect in its petals
Reacted to my touch
By opening into itself
Back to the well
Often that night
'Till the morning caught
The curtain close
Hearts amid the rainlets
Drawn on glass parchment

My high school redux
On my old street
An elm tree stood still
One more time
So I drew a line
With trembling finger
On glass that gave no quarter
To old ideas

A triangle of rifle fire
From rooftop and brush
Changed it all
Then the woman who
Scrambled in pink
Took another wife
And dipped her in oil
The old book opened
To page twenty-one
A mean doorman
Beat a tree with his lens

Perched in solitude
He missed her once again
Drew a perfect circle
With a silver tongue
And whistled up the wind
Trees shivering in the yard
Grainy tape played "Chances Are"

Against tuxedo Joe
Brown skin and black heart
The boutonnière's trade
Broke new ground

An old four-poster
Near the seat of power
With running wheels
That held history close
Defined the lot
This place and that
Not that it mattered
Could have been anywhere
The shift opened true
Dreary they caught the bus
Or train I can't remember

Of leaves that were two-sided
Like all leaves
Of trees that grew in threes
Like few did this one had
Lines that went up and out
Visions that skimmed the skies
Bricks that held rainbows
Once shimmered near
Old grout the answer
That held together the question
Where was I then?

When the old lady died
Dried flowers stayed on
Watching the men wrap her up
Carrying long guns to church
Two was the count
One two one two
Military wariness prevailed
A little cannon prayed too

They said on the news
5,000 birds fell from the sky
In Arkansas near a dry river

Ten thousand fish washed up
Ashore to their ends
Couldn't find the clicker
Fast enough to change
So watched in horror
At cleaning supplies

Razzle dazzle
Holiday time
I hated holidays that
Wouldn't stay put
They ran on and on
One half a million crazy elves
Just finished the dress-up game
And now they're drinking
Again and again
The dogs just came out
To see what I was doing
Pounding the keys to get
A new sound

A policeman's ball
He bounced up and down
Telling me to turn in
Turn around
Stop doing it altogether
But of course I didn't
Listen for one minute
Stole the ball to bounce
It myself that night
The night it all changed
I found you on the Internet
Doing cartwheels through space
Opaque and clear together
Your perfect breast
Clinging to my teeth

Changed a hundred times
This tie or that one
A murderer's suit
I put on over the striped one

Walked down the corner
Cleaning as I went
And singing that song that
Stuck in the sky the clouds
Dance to it dance
While you killed me again
You laid me out
In my Dad's seersucker suit

No matter how much I begged
To know how you did it
And why not that it mattered
As I have already said
You told the answer to a little boy
Related it to a small running girl
Who giggled a response
To my silly query
Shall we take it 'round again
Play roundy-round?
Pirouette and curtsey
For the pretty lady with the
Shaking hands

Anyway I kept looking
Trying to locate a key or lock
A secret hardly shook this town
Seen it all once or twice before
Carnival in town
Posters slapped up
Lawyers lined up
Lik-m-aid, that's a funny name
For a candy you eat
When you're very young
Who thought of that I wonder?
Who even could think that?

Looking over quickly
During set changes
The curtain was stained
Torn from the bottom up
The *Playbill* was in any language

But my own
Unable to read it
I just ate the damn thing
The words whatever they meant
Stuck to the roof of my mouth
And dripped down inside
Bitter to the swallow

Tried to get up and out
Before the airplanes crashed
Killing Bill Evans and hope
Denying my dreams
Ran like hell
Toward the big old river
They built bridge after bridge
But only for pay not travel
Looking at the other side
Part of me wondered
Where was my little girl?

Did some man grab her
Tuck her into his parts?
Cart her away?

I would have lied forever
No we didn't go to France
We never saw the old river
Accordion Joe never played
That theme from the TV
What was that movie?
The one with Fred Astaire
Black and white and back
Color on the fringes
Old paint on my fingers
I just realized they took the door
The one from inside my garage
When they changed the locks
No really it's now gone
The door that I drew on
The secrets of Islam from
A Navy Captain who knew

His crime was caring
They made him sew up our enemy
On a ship five miles offshore
He told me straight
The Koran was five stories
Told 95 times
A good man and a bad one
Different than the Torah
But with the same mother
And where was that door now?
Chopped up for sawdust
To put between the teeth?
Or maybe they're laughing at it
In some University classroom
The man wore a Sox hat
And a Cubs uniform
And the stick figures I drew
Running up and down his arms
Told only the truth.

MOODY'S PUB

1. History

Armory Park on Broadway, on Chicago's bohemian North Side
Built to house the troops that General Sheridan commanded
Trained to put down anarchist insurrection
Needed more swiftly than the men garrisoned up in Lake Forest

A massive structure, now a wonderland
Of humankind's ability to pile bricks over wood
Hulking, most know little of its significance
Men, trained at war, armed and aimed at the city's working class

Ago the streets were mud, and roughed by wheels
But at the gates of the old Armory, straw was always handy
To mat down the stretch where horses had to turn
The wheels tearing the streets for the men close behind

They drilled, mostly Irish and Scots
They swilled beer in the tavern across the street
The uniformed officers hoisting round after round
To steel their blood for the butchery ahead

By stealth the leaders met, their German hands still dark with print
Some brought gunpowder in
The many prayed, and broke their bread
The strikers plotting to make their stand

For they would face them down at Union Square
At the Armour gates, with the carved cow's head and roses
In solid rock, arched over the pathway
While a hundred thousand men walked in clean and walked out bloody

2. Modern Times

In the night, in the thirties and forties
When men grew to know their drink
The drive from down where the money was, then back to the house
Led them down this very street

Later still, when jazz cracked the air
In a dozen night places, behind the Edgewater Beach Hotel
They stretched down the lakefront, to the south Loop
To Bronzeville, Hyde Park and to the South Shore

Your Dad, and mine, would take this same route, to avoid the new road
They built along the lakefront
When the Friday night big band broadcasts
Ceased to sound from the big pink hotel

It was beer gardens in the summertime
Or Hackney's on Harms
But when the snow blew across Loyola Beach, past Mother Mary's arms
It was Moody's Pub for drinks, and burgers and fries

Dead across from the old Armory, we favored it as well
In the in-between seasons, where my Mom would wear a scarf
Yellow, with birds on branches, stretched across her brow
So the windows could stay down, the cool changing air blowing through the car

Moody's would seat you outside, if you demanded it
Even when the snow might be coming
They'd light an outside fire that delighted our eyes
My brother, my sister, and I entranced

We couldn't sit inside at Hackney's
My Mom couldn't stand the jukebox
The Elvis Presley and Peggy Lee
Offensive to her opera-happy ears

We'd swing down to Moody's, and park by the fire
My Dad would wave his hand at the massive Armory
Telling stories of working-class heroes
Who faced down the guard, all roused from their sleep

The Ford Motor plant, where the women braved the lines
Of thugs with bats and clubs and hammers
To bring legs of turkey, and bread and beer
To the desperate men holed up inside

One took a blow, and kept on walking
A song of strength at her lips as she staggered
My Dad would retell the same story
Of working people, strong, facing capital down

We'd shrug at the tales, but the old building
Looming over the brick garden of fire and beer
Always seemed to be endless, and alive
The sounds of boots stored in its bricks and mortar

3. Story Time

That time my Dad and Mom piled us in the car
Late in the 60s, for a spring night called us
Toward the old Broadway haunt
Of your family and mine

You squeezed in between my Mom and my Sis
While I played with the Radio
In the front seat
Of my Dad's massive push-button car

You remember my hand on the radio
But more emphatically
A conversation between Father and Son
Between man and a boy, with hair flowing back

The war raging across our America
About the draft and the boxes carrying our dead
Loaded off of transport planes
At Fort Pendleton, and Bragg and Sheridan too

The same Fort up the Lake
That the Armory supplanted
The need to quell insurgency
From men and women hell-bent on their rights

My Dad, with witnesses around, a family man
Offering to send me to Canada
Or Sweden, farther still
If my draft number was a low one

He was willing to send me away
To keep me from military service, and he a vet
Decorated for radio technology, a signal jammer
Part of the big winning war machine of old

4. *The Gift*
It all swirls around
The memories of those clear crisp nights
When you were a girl, and I was a boy
And danger was in the air, just a breath away

Today I found the Winter and Summer menus of Moody's Pub
The hot drinks changing to wine spritzers and brews
The drawings of the old place classic
Like when we haunted its skinny room and wide garden

I like to think it built
A new ladder in each of our chests
An interior way to climb inside
And build our future selves, with materials from those nights

The hand on the radio
The hand on the spinner
The hulking building where men prepared for battle
The breeze unsuccessful as it passes through the open car windows

Oh old night
Long ago night
You came back to me
On the wings of love, a pure pure gift

The blackness, the wind gusts
The light in everyone's eyes
It flickers now before me
The memory fresh inside

I see us all, we're laughing
We've joined the throng in line
Our cares are all before us
Our thoughts frozen in time.

NATIONAL SECURITY

The District was to be carved from land between waters
The Anacostia, the Potomac, and Rock Creek
A survey revealed that God's providence had consecrated this swath
With fair lines of sight, and fruit trees, and fine soil
America the young was perched on greatness, although predicated on a
    grand lie
That all men were created equally, and treated so
By the great White fathers who claimed this land from the redcoats
With their wigs, their codpieces, their riding crops
Today they'd be welcome at the Anvil or the Bunghole

Great Father Washington had ridden up from Richmond
To command the vast armies of ragged men
And drive the British to the sea
They showed mercy to the prisoners, and fed them well
Unlike the savages whom they drove from these lands
Unlike the slaves whom they beat without mercy
For the redcoats looked like them, and spoke their tongue
They sent them home for Christmas, packed them off
To run a new country in a new world where the land stretched west
For weeks at a time you could wander, never seeing a soul
Up Cumberland, over the Appalachians, and into the Ohio Valley

America needed a nadir, a Rome
To house the armies, and run the courts, and keep the Senate
A room of busy, sweating men, shouting each other down
A grand city was conceived, and a Frenchman named L'Enfant
Engaged to dream up the alabaster city on the banks of all these tributaries
Where the highest ideals, and the lowest instincts
Could comingle on streets so fine and wide, that Paris would turn her head
In admiration of the new configuration of stone, and statuary
Carved out of the wide Virginia quarries

This country, conceived in liberty, for one quarter of her citizens
The trick, counting men in bondage as a percentage of a man
So that electing in this new theocracy looked like something it wasn't
This is still with us today, a legacy of the slave trade
That built the roads, the towns, and the great byways
That dug the canals, and picked the fruit

Suckled the babies, and cooked the meals
And the suffragists and the abolitionists
Who would someday have their way
Could only look on in horror, as the city was carved
From the clay of black hands and black backs
While the women were sold away, to nurse the babes of democracy

L'Enfant was a prissy man, like many of his day
A fine and cultured man, who disdained the new President
And the commissioners assigned to him
Who had befriended a brilliant Black mathematician
Benjamin Banneker, whose calculations and surveying skills
Surpassed even those of this Frenchman, although his pedigree
Included his father's service to Louis XV
True, at age 23, he joined Lafayette's staff
And helped to free the colonies from the Brits
He brought his painting skills, acquired through tutelage at the Louvre
And painted the Virginia General as he ascended the steps to power
One might question his allegiances
For the French hated the Brits, more than anyone, more than God
Who was still mad because of the death marches in India, China, and
    the new world

For the great experiment, the land of highest calling
Was a stage set, a western town, of false fronts
Behind the thin veneer of truth was a pack of lies
That stretched across the eastern crags to the great water
That split the country in half, like a hatchet
Every great work that we can point to, the feats of modern engineering
Built upon these lies, and magnified thousands of times over
The grand boulevards of Columbia, of God's shining city
Soaked with red blood, into the red clay
The bold strokes of the whip upon the backs of men and women
That gave all for her beauty and her majesty

Banneker came from a mixed marriage, and a curious one
His grandmother, an indentured servant named Molly Welsh,
She bought a slave, a brilliant man, who came from the Dogon tribe
Known throughout the diaspora for their skills in astronomy
Which they applied to crop rotation, and irrigation, and land planning
This Banneker was the source material for the beautiful district

That today is our nation's home, its center and seat
From this African man came the mind that organized all of the information
Needed to create such a paradise of greed
A place where war was ordered, where grand laws were written
Where purchase or theft of land, depending on the owners
Would provide a new country with vast tracts
Unending, the birds that flew west
Could flap around the world, it seemed
Before settling on the old trees along the banks of the Potomac

When L'Enfant fled, and took his plans with him
The plans so beautifully articulated the vision of a great city
One where you might find redress
From the slights of commerce and avarice
He had employed this Banneker, the pride of Mr. Ellicot
Who showed young Benjamin the ways of the great mills
Along the fertile Patapsco river
Benjamin fed the men, and studied the planets
Having a Quaker for a friend, he devoured a whole library
Books that he read as a starving man gulps water
Learning the secrets of motion and time, he built a clock
A wooden clock, with elegant working parts
It still would tick today, some three hundred years hence
Had it survived the ravages of time and war

His calculations were so perfect, they have been studied
By students of architecture, and city planning
Who today still marvel at their cunning results
Broad avenues, bisected by cross streets, and dotted with fine squares
Where the young families could picnic and the feisty men could walk
Their backs to old Europe, and their fronts to the west
Their primping, powdered waltz
Provided by this descendant of slavehood and servitude
The genius of the plan, as men marveled across the ocean
When news of the city crossed the Atlantic, and resonated
In the corridors of power from the Thames to the Danube
They didn't know that it was from the mind of Banneker
That all of this grandeur came to pass

Race the underbelly of this all, and still today
The shining city on the banks of these waters where a young

President shines black as coffee
Up out of Chicago, his loyalty questioned
One thousand websites dedicated to his demise
Like the little square dedicated to Banneker, lost amid
L'Enfant Plaza, our leader's removal the subject of countless
Spit and chaw sessions on brutal front porch steps
History waits to be rewritten by the new victors
Who gussied up their message to stir the fears of people
They once worked but now complain for a living
The vast government built by men and women without color
Paying their bills and catching their wrath
The know-nothings now on the march
A few things collected while in the fair city where drama rules
Where Booth leapt from the balcony of the Ford Theater crying
Treason and tearing a flag as he fell, tearing the nation in parts again
His broken ankle the exposed heel of the south, and the bitter minds
    of the North
The rivals now the pallbearers, the North in grief
The South left to its own devices, to pick up the pieces amid
Ruined cities, burnt crops, and broken families

At the spring of Bethesda, which hid the secrets of the young king
Whose frontal lobe and occipital bone had smashed against the
Dallas pavement, his instant widow in a pillbox hat scrambling
To collect the brains of this superior mind as they blew across the back of the
Limo, the driver finally gunning the gas after the deed was complete
The Navy Hospital, with its tower sketched by FDR on a napkin
Never recovering from its shame, the botched autopsy
A litmus test of credulity and of circular blame

Why did they kill these men? One hundred years apart, each took
    his own stand
Against intolerance, against blind hatred, against the bloated bellies of
Black children who mixed paint with their eggs, who left hope at the
Church doors, and grew cold spores of hate in their ravaged souls
The intrigue built into the system, the hillbilly lawyer dragged down by such
Hate, his sexual needs draped over the front pages so we could cluck
At the limits of sanity in the Oval Office
William Jefferson Clinton, often called our "first black President,"
For his earthy ways, and his sad saxophone antics, had offended the same
Men in the box that pulled the strings

It had to swing back to them, to the boots that beat the fields
These secret men not even satisfied with double-digit returns in their
    portfolios
They just wanted to defeat him, at any cost, and, satisfying their
Endless blood lust, they drained the Treasury as soon as they could

When I entered the fair city, a minor victor amid all this drama
I waltzed into the West Wing to claim my prize
And rewarded by the sight of my young Black King, amid the grinning
    Chicago
Bulls, the point guards and the President all smiles
Then upstairs to meet the staff, and see the elegant, cramped rooms
    without
Air, where the First Lady and her staff were planning their days
It all seemed so giddy, the Wednesday night martinis, the conga lines,
Earth, Wind and Fire in the East Wing, Stevie Wonder on the lawn
I should have known instantly that it was all wrong, or too good to be true
I saw the paramilitary men, short and compact, all in black
Their sharpshooting spotters waiting on the White House roof
You could see them with powerful binoculars, scanning the rooftops
Of this crazy town, built so close that a sneeze in the Eisenhower
    Building
Disturbs the National Security staff in the bunkers, six stories below
    the ground

After dancing through the House, I needed a drink
Which they gladly shook for me at The Last Call, under the
    Hay-Adams Hotel
The same place that Barack lived while they fixed up his digs across the
    street
I had only been there five or ten minutes when a man sat on the stool
    next to mine
He had on a green mohair sports coat, a white shirt and a brown tie
But then I noticed that the shoes were all wrong
For rather than wings, or loafers, or saddles, no these were
Special Forces slippers, black and sleek, and clashing with the ensemble
Hastily thrown together, now I devise, to meet me at that very spot
Turns out he was what I thought he was, a spook
An army man who lived six stories down, under the East Wing
He'd popped up on command, to see what was shaking
I'd been in the Capitol dome that morning, and then out to

Bethesda, to the Navy Hospital, to see if it could be made right
By experts concerned about infection, and about healing arts
And how horses might help heal these brave men and women
Their faces stitched together after a roadside bomb had ragged them off
Their souls wounded, even more so, their hands twitching as they
Waited for new orders. I had just met one of them, a kid from
Nebraska, so courteous as he sat by the rusted sculpture in the
Hospital lobby, that proclaimed the unity of our forces, and the
Special role of a corpsman in battle, offering a needle and a cradle
To a man blown apart by gunpowder and cell phones, of wires and guile

This spook sought me out, for I had crossed the magic threshold
And looked up under the nation's skirt
I'd seen the young black and white prince
Who had wrapped our nation's dreams in his strong hands
And had taken them to the hoop, as it were, slam dunking a solid win
For my parents, for Dr. Abernathy and Dr. King, for those
Four little girls who perished in the hater's bomb in Birmingham
For the families that followed Chavez into the lettuce fields to sit down
Risking everything, not just a day's meager wages
For the lunch counter sitters, their hair mauled by Cokes and sugar
The freedom riders, caught in the backs of burning Greyhound buses
On cold southern mornings, and for the women who bled to death from
Back alley aborts, whose car coats were covered with the blood of their
Offspring, torn from them under horrific conditions

The nation's center was in a frenzy of hate and love all at once
New ways to hate, to make it seem so nice, from those who wanted their
Country back. They wanted to get back what had been taken from them
In 1960, in '65 and '68, that was so long ago most didn't remember or
      weren't here
When the heavy lifting happened, in 1957, when we were still two nations
The one a blur of football games, and gin and tonics, and bowling balls
Of stocks and bonds, and GI bills, and college dreams for a new
      generation of
Phone booth crammers, and goldfish swallowers
The other a musty reeking smell, of piss on elevator walls, of a mashed-up
Feeling of choke and bile, of coke-bottle glasses held together by tape
Of Sunday church macaroni, and brimstone prayers of deliverance
Of dogs and water cannons, of Bull Connor and George Corley
      Wallace

And Strom Thurmond on the courthouse steps, all
Before Barack, for he was too young, and from Hawaii, and not too
black for the Joe Bidens of the world, but we remembered, those of us
who grew up in the bosom of The Movement, that this would not last
too long. Men would come packing to public
Meetings within eyeshot of the President, and the nation sighed, as
we'd
Seen it all before, but our world-weary eyes didn't have a forum to tell
this to

Our nation, torn asunder, with liberty for the few, the tax cuts for
Rich, and benefits Cuts for Poor, we shambled like before, as if it
never happened
The millions of women in white dresses, lining up fresh out of buses
from all
Fifty states and territories, the Million Man march, strong men singing
in the buses.
Even this a flawed moment, for the gay men and women had to hide
their rainbows
Lest they be outed in the macho crowd. The Buddha had cried, too, an
unusual thing
For such a sinner/saint, but his tears, stained by cigarettes and brandy,
and his
Earthy ways, rang true for every saint and sinner among us who has
dreams
Shattered and torn, away from the land so labored while born

There's a coda, an end to this song about Columbia, its sinners and
saints
It came to me when a taxi wasn't available, and a bright young man
with a ponytail
Rode up on a rickshaw to take me from the Ellipse to DuPont Circle
He was magnificent, his legs wrapped in black tights, his skinny
bottom and
Muscular back working as he took the cycle uphill from the bottom to
the top
From the District to DuPont, where quiet diplomatic dreams could
live
Driven in Audis, and Beamers, and Benzes, to the quiet rooms where
they plied their

Trade. A historian for the eager rube in the back of the cold
  rickshaw, biting my
Tongue, trying not to say too much, past the Museums, the Spitzer
  Hotel, up the
Grand boulevards, he told me about L'Enfant, and his magic dream,
  for this
Wicked city, and looked back, with a start, when I asked him about
  Banneker
For Benjamin he didn't know, it was all just a rumor anyway—look at
  the *Wiki*
Page, where the word jumps off the screen—rumors abound, what he
  didn't do,
What we can't ever know. I'm sure he wasn't complicit, that he *couldn't*
  know.

The information fed to him from the trough of lies, and fixed up with
  Scholarship for the rabble, who could breathe a sigh of relief—the
  main
Achievements were, then, only basketball and Motown, and a fluke
  election
Of a man who promised change, but could barely deliver
Whose own heel exposed, the man lived across the street from James
  Madison's
Church, but hardly went, and he naively believed that it didn't matter
Tripped him up, worse than Rev. Wright, whose own story so maligned
We'll never remember him as a Navy corpsman, stitching up President
  Johnson
His face smiling from under the surgical cap, his hands true to his craft
A President made well by the man with the devil in his blue eyes and
  black skin.

NINE TANKA POEMS

Manhattan

Full moon in Cancer
Up over Central Park East
Few cabs out early
Breaking silence in cadence
Red lights north and white lights south

Manhattan Redux

Glide walk Fifth The Frick
Picasso's nine-year-old fig
Imagine these rooms
Now lined with red cloth of paint
On wood to stir the blood up

Water Tower

Water tower prose
Praise for the wooden buckets
Perched on many roofs
As far as the eye can see
Water sits over each one

Skyline

The shifting skyline
Is everything you want now
For that one last look
Until all changes again
And it is so different

Nightmare

With night heading here
Just the thought of comfort touch
Keeps me in the game
But when the chasm of dark
Comes my fears take me down slow

Family

It's like day and night
Switch places like old cousins
Did this at dinner once
What we didn't expect then
Was the hot for cold it left

Interior

A collection dear
Kept from view but never far
My heart! Does covet
Single scenes together make
A film that plays back our life

The New Me

Seeing where I fit
New everyday encounters
Are the centerpiece
A life without hate just love
Our world such a planet

Reba Place

Where lilacs once grew
Forsythia also gone
That corner tot lot
Was where I took my children
Strange how one's life deck is cut

1942 NEBENZAHL REDUX

Ruth

It has been since April when the curtain
Tightened the final tight
Police roundups in the street were now
Common, although each time the
Proud, Flemish men who served the
Antwerpen force exceeded even their
Master's request for Jews, by several
Hundred each night
With roundups into June
Their prowess proof of Northern might

Seymour

The heat of August guaranteed that the film
Colony was near-empty, but the kitchen-sink
Script of *Hitler's Madman* had been
Rescued from the bigs at MGM, a poverty-row
Find rushed into rewrite and a blistering
Sun passed over it all, the film flourished and grew
A loosening of the tight
Under the same menacing moon
And the same endless night

David

Lies told to young David, a train bound
To the sea, a relocation of foreign blood
For a grateful Cardinal, who washed his hands
Twice each night as his meal was laid out
Before his stern watch and gaze
His books opened, fingered but not consulted, his
Confessor absent, his moral compass atilt
Convoys of human shock and fright
Assembled at the docks at noon
Loaded, and counted, and at *Mechelen* by night

An Army crease, a polish and pack, my
Father took his service to Florida to break
Codes, and jam radio broadcasts with even
Bigger broadcasts, his mechanical genius
Entry to officers' school, the drilling and the
Politics, the martini in the cool room, the
Olives and pickled onions and a watchful eye
Pumped, arm-wrestling, ranking other strong men
His young vision, its limited sight
Retiring in the heat of early eve to his room
Stripped of his sorrows, his loneliness, his fright

Myriam

Mimi always having to pee, holding it
Day into night into day into year into year
Terror under floor, at the threshold each turn
Of Mother's visit, the smell of fresh baked
Bread, chill of terror at night, as Cousins, uncles, rabbis are
Caught, and forced to experience unknowable
Horror, in the *Antechamber of Death*, down
Quiet Streets with tidy trees, rimmed with
Iron, poking downward, at people level
Menacing in the eye, in Mother's protective sight
Under the Cross, the lowlands did rune
Our family splintered, torn, mad in fright

Heinrich

A gentleman's walk in August, across the
Diamond district, to the station, one last
Look at the shop. How old must one man be
To walk this walk, from the shop to the sea, then
By a train, for a land far away?

a. Forget that they beat him with posts
Forget that he was relieved of his coat,
Star removed, taken to the lice room for
Safekeeping

b. Forget that they mocked him, his flesh and
Beard, his nine decades of receding manhood
His dignity, and his pride, and, finally, he gave over his
Self, to be erased and forgotten, to be ever
Lost to us

c. Forget that they took him, laughing, wildly gesturing
The old man standing silently by the docks with his
Holy Books in hand

d. We don't ever, ever forget.

For Amelia, Aria, Ian and Zarah, for Jay Jay and Leyla

1942 was a bad year for our family
For the world, for the *soul* of the Western World,
For *God's* soul, for the whole world and each and every
Tree and garden and blossom and pond
For young men and old women, for
Poets and pederasts, for God and goddess alike
The evil was unleashed like a technoblitz, a
Tsunami of organizational might
Of timetables, and schedules, of rules of right
That took away the human glow
Bulb by blessed bulb, until no longer could it
Burn, or even bring a filament up to light

That's when strong people found their knees
On cool stones, on wooden rows of pews

Of grass in green and of dirt in black
Of wax, and flame, and of utter wretched shame
Imagine that there are no pebbles to be found, to be
Softened under old skin, to be
Laid on our stones, broad and tall, and shady on
Bright summer mornings
When reality dawns, the sweaty jerk up from sleep
To wake, to crawling fright
The radio in the background, an otherwise still
And evil, evil Night.

NOTHING TO UNDO

The message appeared again on my iPhone
"Nothing To Undo"
I stared at it dumbly, blankly
Precisely because there was *so much* to undo
So much that could never be undone
And then the word "cancel" appeared under that
Adding to my confusion
What should I cancel?
Was that referring to future undos
That I hadn't yet done?

For starters I would have stayed away from the allure of
My father's coin collection that I pilfered when I was six
Enriching the guy at the Main Street cigar store
I think he must have had a name for me
Among his orange Nehi cohorts
When I sauntered in with a Morgan or a walking half
To buy candy model cars baseball cards
With my friends it's all on me I'm the house today

The night that I threw bleach at Lizzie Bloom
At our hippie summer camp
We were all running around unrestrained
Peak beauty August night Michigan shores
Was it a convoluted hide and seek?
Can't recall the specifics of the game
Lots of kids we were thirteen
But at the Youthie Bathhouse I grabbed
A bucket and threw it at Lizzie
Well it hit her in the face Thank god it was diluted
In modern grownup time she was a substitute teacher at my
Daughter's school and when I heard that my
Bag of bones heaved
I'd gladly take that night back

From my preverbal life I'm desperate to undo
Whatever it was that happened
That turned some regular chummy nights
When I could be in a tightly made bed
With ironed p.j.'s and the sound of the

Elevated train cars turning in the rail yard
Ten blocks away
No, some horror of violence was my gift
To have and to hold even though I don't
Know the remembered only the imagined
Curve of this one
The terror came at night
Of this I am now sure
On the end of a lemon peel
An offhand punch
From a bartending pugilist
Passing on the stairs did he
Stick out his tongue at me?
He had been in the Army and
I was in diapers
Fair fucking fight

Let me tell you Richard Nixon there's
Plenty to undo
Lots to reconcile and time about out
So you're dead heard that excuse before
We grew and our p.j.'s grew with us
The lamps changed as did the carpet
The kitchens went all the way from
White to avocado to walnut to chrome
There's the societal redo list
There's my brother waiting for the sheriff
To take his stuff away
There's waiting forty years
To fall in love with you
All that I'd undo, in a heartbeat, if I could

OCTOBER'S SUIT

I walked down Maple Avenue right past you
You were eight, and I was ten
I was going to the Y, you were standing in front
Of the big double deep courtyard brick building on the
East Side of the street. You gave me a goofy look
Your eyes sparkled, and you did that You Are Crazy
Thing with your finger in a circle around your
Ear. You were going somewhere, as well, but I
Didn't Notice. But well when I was past, you
Dashed across the street, heading straight for your
Trees, and for the park where you could lay across a
Shadow and travel up into that canopy, out above its whispering
Boughs, over the water and farmland to marble
Halls and to mountains of books, overflowing like
Water against stairs, tables, shelves, fireplaces, a
Babel of words, colors, and inner music, a
Window of whirl, of luminous fabrics, of
Trail away on wisps of wind in October's suit of
Silver against the clear sky, and fall's Yellow, Red and Brown.

OPEN HEART

In the basement there is a bird
Trapped down there, thought it was a crow
Behind a discarded couch, flapping its big
Meat-eating wings in anger and despair
Screwed up my courage, I'm afraid of birds
When they're big/strong flesh-eating
They fly and God knows I can't
I can only protect my eyes with my arms

But the bird that came out from behind the couch
In this dark basement day
Is a hummingbird beating its wings
A thousand times a minute
A red crest, and sending wind around
From the furious life force that gave it flight
I coaxed the little bird up the stairs
And out into the open air through the kitchen door

Realized that the bird is my soul
Released from the basement, my despair
Turning, sure as the earth does
From anger to hope, from trapped to free
Talking with you, about the house
How the house is me
The basement is the place where my
Wires are stored, my mechanicals

So the kitchen is my heart
Where I provide nourishment for my family
The hearth my soul where I heat the night
The bedroom my body
Where I love and bleed
The study, my books lined on shelves
My mind, where I dream and work
The garden my scales and arpeggios
Where I make music for the air to feel

Finding that bird, and letting it go
Watching it fly into the cool morning air

Remembering other hummingbirds in my life
That I marveled at, their hard work for a drop of nectar
Thinking in wonderment at the red crest and coat
The determination to stay alive
To find solace in the tiny drops
Of nectar that we need to survive

That bird now soaring
Its bird's eye seeing all that is below
The town that I grew up in
The streets that I skipped down
Yes were raised for service
Born to help, to see and feel
Now free, my soul comes right back
To find its rightful place
And that little bird is
A perfect open heart
Of translucent love and truth

PIÑATA OR KRISTALLNACHT?

First let me ask for a quiet moment to think about the people of Homs
In Syria, where women and children are being systematically
Exterminated in the streets today right now
As we sit down for our very fine steaks and the good wine
And adjust the heaters and the quilts and the volume on the set

The question as posed on a child's anniversary
Every day is a silent anniversary
Of the rage and rampage of hate
That we let ourselves down into each year when
We honor the Jewish children killed in Austria in 1945 in barbaric fashion

Liberation day coming on an improbable story of US soldiers
Walking the alpine riverbanks in search of ordinance
Clearing the path for tanks and jeeps and marching troops for
General Patton's army of weary men insane with saving the world
Insane with getting back to the States

Just as the men had to wait out the spring and the frozen waters
So we wait until May, right at the end of the War
When the two last camps in Europe fell into Allied hands
The slaves and skeletons collapsing into the tough American arms
The men slack and shell-shocked at the sight of walking corpses

When we go to the camp, and cover ourselves with dust
We bring flowers in our fingers clay-baked flowers shells and hearts
They are sewn into a quilt of clay and cloth and teeth and flowers
And laid beside the priests and the hard rocks at the crematorium
How these ceramic souls long to rest in the grass near the roadway!

For we come from New York, from Chicago we
Follow those tough US Army men that walked the river that May morning
In 1945 when the Russians were closing in from Prague
The Nazis who ran the slave camps for Messerschmitt
Wanted American jailers, and sought them out

Our descent nearly seventy years later to the valley of Gusen
A soft parade of history seekers, of soul prayers, of right makers,
Of reflection Bearers, of peace pledgers, wearing our families' colors
Proud and humble children of freedom fighters
Blood related to those crushed in the tunnels near the orchards at Gusen

The horror of war, and the horror of hate combined
Leaving the innocent and the righteous and the survivors and the liberators
In an angel circle over the descendants who rise and shine in this hard
    place
To bake their daily bread, and live their lives for
To live is to be human is to try is to think and remember and breathe

For our teachers—Stanley and Jimmy, and the other survivors—
    tell a story different
Of the beauty of each new day even from under brutal the boot of
    death
This is hard to understand and accept, for we white Americans are a
    privileged people
Used to arguing with civil servants
And flipping the bird to fellow drivers on our clogged motorways

It took some Ivy League kids this week at a Holocaust literature reun-
ion
Nervously touching each other and eating cookies and strawberries
In Philadelphia PA where so much of our own liberation story is born
They set my soul soaring making new clay hearts to take to the Camp
And lay next to the rescued souls already there soaking up the frozen sun

Breathe and read and talk about the things that hurt
Soak the hurt away with kisses and laughter and nervous gallows humor
Tell the story read and breathe and study and talk about the things that
Hurt and kiss away the laughter with pain we feel the story
Demands laughter with tears a piñata with my Kristallnacht please

PLUTO

Pluto must have come in with the morning light
Settled over the house like a birdcage shroud
Heavy fabric window treatments blocking out
Breathing thinking solving all of a sudden
My brain worked slower in a pathetic surrender
And in building an Indian Scout fire in the hallway
To illuminate the situation and the room
There was little the human mind could do to prevail

Walking to the car I could feel the Plutonian
Pull in my legs as I strode
Like telling the temperature from cicadas I can tell
Time of day from Chicago Avenue traffic
The minutes increasing as truck taxi and cop traffic pick up
Finally I'm home settled in with the newspapers and cups
That live in my car reminding me of the other days I was living
But driving through the astrolandscapes that now guide me
I noticed many changes to my routine map of travel

Every light pole had a Smurf perched on it that was odd
Some corner buildings had 30's plaster statues they could be
1. Indian Man (So. Pulaski Avenue) 2. Space Hot Dogs (Devon at Nagle)
Indian Man now selling eyewear and services "I See Now How"
Hot Dog man and woman selling hot dogs
Now not the movie Smurf but a real live one
And of course all the other animated, now-come-to-life figures
That dominate my teetering daymare nightdream that lives
By placing inside my head a projection machine
Projecting false images all day alone
That medication never saw or knew or offered a cure

Most improbable and splendid of all
The center of town was stuffed full of chipped ice
In a fantastic array of colors and animals we'd never seen
There was burrowing into the ice, which was gooey and warm
By floaters who came in on the late train and were planning
Early exits (maybe that's what they were looking for)
I knew the day was lost but came to calm myself
Joining the others I sat in a cave of sugar ice

Someone made it like a Barnes and Noble
I personally arranged my coffee, newspaper and beat poetry
Pluto had the floor, but we had the day

Rainbow Sherbet

Rainbow Sherbet had been thinking for weeks about moving farther up the coast since the storms settled; she had the distinct advantage of being able to envision the exact spot that she would build on, and had thought herself a deed to the land perched at the end of a long peninsula where the suns sank into the blue water at day's end with a sigh. It was with some satisfaction that she had these thoughts, which nonetheless troubled her again at mid-evening so that she needed an extra wafer of calming soap for her bath. Quickly releasing the troubles, her mind was soon back at work on deeds and trusts and she racked up a large invoice before drying herself on the long porch that wrapped the west side of her home on the eager sea.

Her grandmother had been a Captain in the war between People and Beasts, and Man, and, after the People and Beasts had prevailed, and we know so well how nicely they treated their captives after victory that we don't need to recall such things here, the estate on the eager sea had been passed to Rainbow's parents and then to her, although she was now considering this move north for redemptive reasons. Rainbow's particular and singular genius had been to revise real estate into a kinetic system of thought-egaletaria, which she had then honed to suffice her own control over vast tracts of land that she fancied and that now encompassed the swath called *Frothia* which made her the envy of her colleagues and brought less sleep than imagined to her eyes, hence the thoughts of relocation which intruded occasionally at the same hours.

It had been years since she visited what was left of the jutting land that the Men had retreated to, although she responded to every appeal to assist them in their plight and had built schools and groves and named a center for bathing and learning after Acorn Sequoia, whom she had admired since childhood and had welcomed back after his long sojourn to the southlands where he had learned to understand the nature of things and had built his own center for beast comfort, which was pictured on the cover of every paper tablet published some years ago along with a striking likeness of his face, which she had noticed and collected copies of pending his return.

Still, she thought that a visit to the old country, for this is how she regarded the land over there where unwashed babies were held high each time one of the People passed, would be a good idea, if only to provide her with a needed change of thought and a visit to the old museums that she had protected with a twist of her mind for so many years. She had been collecting things to distribute for such a trip for ten years in an outbuilding at the front of the property, for charity had been her credo and she intended to make quite an impression in the small quarter that bore her grandmother's name just inside the gates to *Francisco*, where she had gone to school and where her memories were stored in a round stone building under twenty-four hour guard by loyal sentries.

Watching her thoughts cascade down her cerebral cortex, she had come to a startling conclusion that a history, true and deep, of the troubles that had led to the great conflict and its resolution had been attempted unsuccessfully, and often, and that she had within her the power of recollection and understanding to undertake such a task, vast as it might be, and so she set out to do this, by gathering at first many pens and papers and engaging in nights of remembering that were sleepless but rewarding, for in just a few weeks she had accumulated an outline of which she was quite proud and which roughly held the story of the past sixty-five years within its spine. This was transferred to thought-disc, and stored in the central library of thought that, not by coincidence, held her father's name, but she was fond of the actual writings and drawings and scribbles that presaged the draft and so kept these around her, finally committing them to decorated boxes stacked upon a series of shelves in her upper study whose large windows afforded her a vista of pines, rock and water that stretched west and north against her home and led to the homes of her children and their own offspring, marked by both trail and road that she remembered well helping her parents to plan and clear that long summer that the beasts has stirred and first asked for more room and then wandered away.

It had been a misty spring season, typical of sea haunts of the north, but the suns had finally beaten back the rolling clouds and Rainbow had succumbed once again to the planting urges that had accompanied each turn of the year since she could recall breathing; for this she was uniquely prepared and had set about to recultivate the large garden that had grown along the seaside of the home, bejeweled with seating coves and wandering lanes that held fragrant surprise at every twist and turn. Her mind had rearranged the garden several times over the past decade but this she finally realized was not quite fair, for she enjoyed the battle with nature and so resumed it this spring with nothing but her hands, a strong garden trowel and seed packets, which had arrived from oversea lands that she fancied and that reminded her of her earlier youthful travels and set her mind at an ease of wander. Soon her work was apparent and the news of the regardening spread along the fortunate coast, so that she was daily receiving visits of eager neighbors and relations who sought the immense lanes and wandering paths with their boughs, flowers and fruits that displayed such color and spewed such fragrances as to bowl over the imagination with adoration and exhaust the senses. When she presently grew tired of such traffic, she posted a schedule at her gates of viewing and wandering times, and at such hours served cool drink and fed the crowds that now came in an orderly fashion with slices of the garden's bounty; she had long ago learned the gardener's trick of instant replacement so that a picked meal regrew within minutes of digestion, and doubled in size, hence affording her a dowry of nutrition that she willingly shared with any and all visitors regardless of lineage or disposition.

Armed with simple tools, Rainbow spent quiet days in reflection as the spring turned riotously toward the crown of summer. Being the year of her content, she took lathers of time to weed out the many thoughts that crowded her mind on the cool to warm days that defined this time of year, plucking her way through the garden regimen and using, to full advantage, the cross-hairs afforded by double sun rises, arcs, and sets to fully exploit the tender mercies of her garden's joys. Oft she would languish on a solitary task that, instead of the usual five minutes, took all morning to accomplish, her head hot with sun and thought, although focused and not aimless, reflecting on a particular passage of life and history that she struggled to fit into what she had originally hoped would be a linear distribution of facts and figures that summed up the whole of her story. For she was struggling, mightily it seemed to her inner eye, with the trajectory of story that added up to the goods of history, and would be remembered after her vast tract of words and images amounted to truth. There was the tricky problem of the middle period, she knew, when she was certainly not a patriot; no, she had consorted with the side of the Men, had wallowed in their struggle, had taken their cry as her own in innocent romance; there were hard days when she either walked the thin line of traitorism or crossed it altogether. This she would have to right, in some elegant and explainable fashion, if history as she remembered it would become tract and dictum, leading the following generation into understanding and into correct behavior as revealed by her later years of realized truth and right. It was all of a piece, one that she thought had been digested well in advance, but that in curiosity came back and again upon her thoughts in ways that held surprise and also threatened her; she surrounded herself more and more often with a ritual icon of the past, a medal or coin or pin, that she hoped would right such mental gymnastics and give comfort and not broker fear on days when the ground seemed to swell toward her lurching hands.

RAYS OF NIGHTFALL

Now I sink into what I thought I left behind
    Reminding that the circle is a sort of cyclone
Sweeping up the items we cast away now they
    Trail behind us connected or free they still come
On the edge of every lip about to speak or forever
    Hold the peace close it consumes and overwhelms
Remembering so and positioning to live through this
    Every time a battle of nerves, societal nerves
A community nervousness that descends and hope that
    Transcends all the racket and clutter in front of me
My gray and excellent mind rattles with the rays of nightfall

REALLY BLIND

You can't see that Mona Lisa was a man?
Gian Giacomo Caprotti was his name
He was da Vinci's assistant
They had an "ambiguous relationship"
Meaning that Caprotti mixed more than
Paints for the Master

I always thought she had that drag queen quality
That she shaved
That the special glow that has been marveled over
Was a knowledge that she offered a comfort to
Leonardo that Lisa Gheradini, his wife, never knew

Imagine the shock in American schools
In art class, when they finally rip off the
Brown cloak that Lisa is wearing
And reveal Caprotti's smooth boy-like chest
His rippling muscles, his soft balls?

That'll turn the art world on its ear
Rothko was a Hopi
Brancusi was a catcher for the New York Yankees
Mondrian collected S & H stamps
Whistler liked country and western music
Titian had bathroom issues
Picasso liked dick, too

Look at Angel Incarnate, and St. John the Baptist
Same soft eyes, pudgy mouth, strange smile
As the Mona Lisa, and that's clearly Caprotti
Ginsberg would be ecstatic this morning
Would have held Peter Orlovsky's hand at breakfast
The whole world "shocked"
But at the Louvre, there is a cry
From the officers of the great museum

You see, even in modern France
If you are gay, and rich, and a man
Then you have a wife, a young woman on the side

And then your gay boy lover
Hiding behind your mistress, a double beard
You never sleep with your wife
And you take your mistress to the Opera
Finally making love with your boyfriend
In the back of your car

The art world has always been a flimsy screen
Behind which the strength of capital markets
Can exercise its options
We like because we are told
This week it's El Lissitzky
Let's collect that!
Next week we'll find an unknown
Wisconsin artist
Who made India-ink splatters
On beaver pelts
That'll be the rage

But Leonardo, liking boys?
That's like Harold Washington in bra and panties
That painting got arrested
At Chicago's Art Institute
The boys in blue, who hated Mayor Harold
Anyway, they handcuffed the painting
And took it away
Those were heady days, with
Mapplethorpe's beautiful silver gelatin prints
Covered with velvet cloth, so one had to
Lift them to see those masterful looks at
Love

We'd prefer an alphabetical museum
A-Z with a good audio tour
With stuff we can understand
He played shortstop, he batted .300
He was beaten by his mother
He was a saint
Etc.
Then way in the back
There would be a special section

Over here, one painting by an African American
Over there, a canvas or two by a woman
Oh, and here, this one is by Yoko Ono
Remember her, she broke up the Beatles

Ripe with Juice

Trees replete fruit + meat
      Skies' swollen waters gather
Candy chrome light dawn of god's + filament
      Human eyes search for shelter
We don't know why we run
      But we run pell-mell into the
Morning each color bursting with
      Meaning each laden with truth
The Human politic ripe with juice
      Meaning liquor sweet drink
Not the drunk kind the lay down and swoon
      Kind of day of immobile thought
These callow days before the cold blood ones
      Our salad youth for sweet remembering

SAMU

Striking, handsome, brave, hard-working
These are the words that described Samuel
Samu, my great-grandfather Sam
Whom, my father said, came over from Hungary
About 1880, alone, from a family of Innkeepers
Who built a small American family, an American
Life, and Never Looked Back to the old country behind

I have that sepia-toned three shot—grandfather, father
And son, my father so bright and cheerful-looking
That his face is ready to burst out of the frame
My grandfather, Herbert, almost Chinese looking
His smile so up in his face that there was no place
For his eyebrows to go, no up available higher than the
Up already in use, the face so stretched out

Growing up, we never heard about Sam from Dad
He couldn't stand his own father, Herbert, who
Having stolen the family business in 1942
When Irv went into the Signal Corps in Ft. Monmouth,
New Jersey, to learn the officer's trade
The ironing, the military corners, the old titles,
Herbert sold it all and went to Los Angeles
Where he then had his own orange tree

Where Sayde played bridge, and mahjong
That Chinese game that swept the nation
Is that why Sam boarded the steamer
That brought him to Ellis Island? Why he took the ride on
The train that chugged through Harper's Ferry
Spewing black soot at three o'clock a.m.
On its way to Cleveland via Pittsburgh
Its final breakfast destination new Chicago

I imagine he couldn't sleep that first time
America opening out in front of the steam engine
Whistling by the open car window between
The dining car and the coach seats
A fine train, we know trains

We've traveled first class before
Between Budapest and Brussels and up
To old Antwerpen, where Hermann set up shop

But this train was different
It was more muscular
It chewed up track across the Ohio Valley
And sounded its name against the graying night wind
"I'm coming, I'm coming, I'm coming,"
America's night train, searing the trees
Whopping through dozens of small towns
Where the folks had come out, like they did
Every night, to see the train steam through
On its way west, to Indian country and open sky

Sam had picked up a wife in New York
Gussie was a fine woman
They stood together between the cars
As the train flew west
Their future before them, literally, figuratively
They stood through the night, the dawn
Coming as they crawled across Indiana
The eastern sky streaked with red, then gold

Sam forgot all about the past that first year
He folded it up like a kite going away for the winter
Reduced to its smallest size, and stuffed on a cold shelf
Stored with twine wrapped around its length
In America where anything and everything could happen
Fantastic things, really, outsized in comparison
To Old Country ways
Here there were hot air balloons, and crisp porters
And warm candy, sold in paper, that stuck to your teeth
And to your hands

Chicago was grand, where it was okay
For a man to sleep on the lakefront on hot nights
In the winter there was coal heat, and electric lights
Strung down every street
The heat of breathing, and singing
Drinking songs into the night

Irish, German, Russian, Polish men singing
They all made him tremble when they
Strode past, Sam trying to become
Very small then

For his journey, from Galicia to Ungvár
From Mother to Father
From poverty to poorer
To Belgium, then, and America
Had taught him elemental things
We were still a people then under
The thumb of men on horseback
Who could knock you off the sidewalk
To the street, laughing
For a lark on a day with little promise

But mostly men were under the thumb
Of capital, of the brutal must work of
Broken backs and busted fingers
Fourteen hours a day, in a dim room
Three breaks, and a meal
A water boy, and a reader
Telling tales to pass the time
Thread, stitch, under, thread, stitch
And under again, the watchful eyes
Always peering, always knowing

Sam would shrug it all off
His keen mind purposeful each day
Counting what he saved
Listing what he collected
Planning for the day
That his son would be born
That his grandson would sparkle in the picture
That his blessed great-grandson
Would run down a flowered hillside
Without the sense to wear shoes, in the mud
Filled with fantastic music, and dressed
Like a prince in the middle ages

Free in America
Free to be dead flat-busted
To be a commie, or join a motorcycle gang
Or draw shoes for the Saturday Evening Post
Free to be trouble for everyone you met
To spit, and wrangle up some noise
Drinking all day, down on your luck
Free to walk across the street
Tell them you're a Christian
Let's start all over again

Sam arriving in Chicago, the old onion swamp
Reborn to be man's greatest city
Its shining city on the plains
On the cold, unforgiving prairie
Its mountain of terra cotta dreams
To challenge Paris, and Rome and St. Petersburg
Its unmatched lake promenade
A jewel of twenty-seven miles
Green by day, and alive by night
With a thousand rocking boats
Anchored along its welcoming shores

I saw a picture of Sammy where he looked like a cowboy
His mustache combed just right, but a fire
In his eyes, soft and hard at the same time
He looked proud and happy
His clothes fit him snug and tight
With a vest, and a pocket watch,
And a cravat folded across his neck
But now I've learned that often the photographer
Would rent the clothes that looked so fine
To impress the people in the old country

It's a who knows, a tossup
Dad's Army discharge papers talk about a factory
Sam's dress factory
Where one hundred men worked, there at seven bells
Every morning, Sam standing in the doorway
Knowing every man who walked in that door
Knowing some from Galicia

Their Dad saying, "Son, look up that
Samu Nebenzahl in Chicago, he'll give you a trade."

But it could just as easily have been lights out
Curtains for Sam and his family
First Chicago burned, its wooden framed
Homes a place for flame to leap
Across the water the fire did travel
Men open-mouthed in astonishment
For this conflagration changed everything
Rich men to poor
Landowners to paupers
The fortunate men rich who had just shipped enough
Lumber to Chicago to rebuild the whole city

And then, from the depths of the fire
Of that sooty despair, the city did rise
An alabaster city on south was consecrated
The white city, and Sam would have packed
His family, for an all-day journey
On the South Shore Elevated Line
Where a White Man could stroll free on the midway
And see a Black Man, from deepest Africa
Living in a cage, while the ladies and gents of Chicago
Walked by in their Sunday finest

Sam would have given up his seat
When the train passed through the Loop
To a crowd of young women going to the Fair
Their carefree ways, the glint of teeth against lips
And the sight of a bare calf against a lace shoe
Made him blush, for he was raised to look away
When his sister Rifka took to the bath
And he stammered, I imagine, and Gussie grimaced
At the baffling mirth of these young American girls
Their laughter as threatening as the thundering of jackboots
To Sam's pious mind

For they were still Hebrews, unmistakably so
With their strange ways
They still meekly stepped aside

And Into the mud
When the finer people walked by
Their impossibly noble features
Reminding Samu and his brood
Of their own darkness, and of the smells
That came from Hebrew homes
The chanting, the candles, the covering of eyes
The fumbling ways that he could not explain

Hard work had its rewards
And Sam worked hard, around the turn of the week
Sometimes not stopping at the Sabbath
For the orders, when they came, must be filled
So that more orders could be ordered,
And filled, and delivered
To Maxwell Street, to Roosevelt Road,
To Betty's of Winnetka
To the Black Belt, with its Finkelstein's,
Its Portnoy's Shoes, and Issac's Hat Shop

It comes as no surprise
That Sam and Gussie, and then Herbert and Sayde
Joined Temple Sholom, then fondly referred to
As the "*Church on the Lake*," where
Rabbi Englehard would give expansive book lectures
So fine, so high and mighty
The German Jews thought they were in church
They sat bolt upright on hard wooden benches
Without a thought they recited The Lord's Prayer
From the New Testament, as if it were their own

The *schul* and its nine-story Moorish outline
Stark against the lake sky
The lines of self-loathing mashed up against the
Sheridan Road doors
Carved to remind those who entered
That Issac was *bound*
Before he sold hats to negroes
Before he danced to Benny Goodman's clarinet
Staring up the fire escape
Now a part of every Chicago cold-water flat

The American dream always within sight
And always a little out of reach
It sounded like you could buy a mansion at those prices
But then the reality of those incredible five-cent steaks
Tempered by the memory of wages so low
That keeping bread and butter and milk
Was a struggle, hard to imagine
In the land of endless milk and honey

Fortunate Sam, who had one son
More than his nephew Adolf, who was barren
Or so his letters would imply
The mail would stack up, and the
"Please, Uncle" requests would wait
For a weekend moment when the
Fortunate American Man
Could send pennies to Europe
So that the family could eat
And so that Sam could sleep next to Gussie
His suspenders hanging behind the door

Sam was furious
Irv had gone to college, the first one
So proud, but then quickly to flare
At his grandson's audacity
To wear the red armband, and sing the
Dreaded songs
That sounded down the great boulevards of Moscow
In the winter of 1917
Sam, having given all
To be on rung number 4,447, but to be looking
Up, up to where America got easier
Couldn't abide by this breach

So that year Irv was yanked out of college
They said that Herbert was sick
But Sam was still strong, and running the factory
Those hundred men turning out suits and dresses
I think they pulled Irv back
To remind him not to get too fast too soon
Too far into the America they found

They created a three-act play in which, at the end
He was back where they had started

By the time I came along Irv had solved the puzzle
He put the steaks on the grill, and sliced the lemon
And wore a short-sleeved shirt on a summer night
He wasn't worried about the Crown Prince
Declaring that his assets were null and void
He was already plotting the overthrow of the
Land that nurtured his people
Gave them solace from the wounds of old Europe
Bound up their wounds, the world's wounds
So great was her promise

I like to think that Sam forged ahead
Lived through his son's myopia
Lived past his grandson's radicalism
Lived from the time of the buggy to the
Splitting of the atom under Stagg Field
Lived to be more or less a Jew again
Listening to book lectures on Sunday morning
He took this leap and lived from 1860 until 1940
To see the curve of a world quite different from the old model
He gave birth to me, to my world
Everything that is possible for me flows from Samu!
And from that day he walked up the plank in Antwerp
And boarded that steamer,
And sailed far, far away.

SMOOTH ROUND BALL

Wish I could smooth round ball bounce it again
Will it so to run Ridge to Maple down the hill so fast
Cresting around corners trees guard the way for me
Always in the back of thinking the memory of a street sign
Plum against my head skin blood playlets the order
Of that day

So thinking these remembers the slight sense of twilight shimmer
Old evenings way home from Valencia grand theater war movie
My shadows playing down clean alleyways
My gait the sound of my shoes
The kick up of my running play thoughts unfolding
All night long

Just came in and flung the body I'm in down
Without care or placement fall into some odd places
Sometimes to wake up in these poses found after abandon
Was a head scratch a tossup of awake faith
The gut check a reality glance all it is across the room
Checking myself out

Oddity the time and mutual thought symposium
Our inc. was formed between streets we lived I still live
Looking at things looking at Bronzeville in the rain
Maps and Mapquest and moved monuments aside
That was the weekend we danced to the *Stylistics*
In my kitchen

From around these parts hardly gets it perimeter
Not bull's-eye circle vision of "I see and I was there"
Not acquired but all the same real the feelings of chance
With an odd zone of few and a bet that can't quit
It's aiming for us pure and square it found us
In its gaze

Giving in to the news left running in the inkwells
Too late to print or type or cast into the hell frenzy
Take that photo and swing it around and add some sass
A man in a dragon jacket silk in the night on rooftops
Can be clicked or tagged at will and thrown all his chops aside
'Round the world.

SATIN DOLL

Sitting at the top of a carpeted step
Dreamland time floating back
To 1962 the year we spent getting
Under our desks at Central School

I used that upper step in the front staircase
It was my perch
An invisible zone
I was never noticed there

A huge ball of tinglefeel would
Descend slowly upon the eight-year-old boy
Of wool and cool steel and prickly plastic
It conked me out by lulling rolling, rubbing

My arms felt enormously increased
Every nerve a tension-release pump
Now I know there is a word for this
But then words meant little as the skin crawled

Here in the sartorial wisdom of six decades
Things that seemed mysterious and without
Anchor in our world can be conjured
By electric scope we can see the outline of truth

But back then that world was ultra linear and
Omni oeuvre at the same moment
It had everything all at once you could
Hold the whole world in your hands, breathing

Fall's grace and the moist ground leave thought open
To think these things it takes this day of solemn stare
Remembering, blissfully the blanket of kinetic charges
Coming over me like a quick summer storm before supper

SOMERSET NIGHTFALL

Fastness across hushful eventide
Quay eddy half a foot of channel
Cinereal upon the din now

Halfraw men's battles
Marred still in dark coppice
Roused in bloody élan vital

Hail comic the fallen trice
Misbegot his Damocles threat
Digits ever present on rangy phalanges

Natality to necrosis
Copse firth bosk tempest
Palter in adventitious caisson

THE BEAR WITHIN

Imagine how strange and powerful to enter a room and find a
Polar Bear standing calm as day there! A big animal, they get to
Nine hundred pounds in a year
White as the sun burns hot, they are the most powerful predators
On this earth
But this bear was casually in the back room
Carrying a pair of sewing shears
In his big paw, with the black claws and the pink pads
You must have been startled, what would he do next, talk?
But his red eyes and wet lips told you something about
His gentle spirit, or else he would have/could have made
Short work of your human flesh
This bear stood on his hind legs, like an enormous man
The rocks carved from the glaciers that came down the Hudson
Outlined through the windows behind him
Now I know Polar Bears, they have a very distinctive smell
But this one was different, more so than we've already established
For not only did he stand ever so gently on his hind legs
Not rocking, not reaching upward to take or catch something
Even stranger still, he reached out his massive mitt
And like a deft tailor, one schooled in forms and patterns so well
That he no longer required them,
He cut through a long red ribbon that spun in the air between you
Between you and the bear
And maybe you caught a smell of him
Not the typical stench of a bear, half to scare you, and half to
Mock you as he sliced through your gullet
But an odor of dried flowers, and chamomile teas, and cut grass he
Exuded, a familiar yet old smell, one that you remembered faintly from
Your great-grandmother's house on Wilder Street
Startled to see him, you stepped back, but his eyes drew you closer still
Into the room, your fingers reached out to catch the ribbon as it
Floated to the floor
Now in two pieces, the ribbon flashed so red against his white belly
His frame filling the room top to bottom, his breath hot against the
Winter night
Not everyone gets a bear visit, and few, if any, survive them when they do
But this bear turned, and walked straight through your earthly walls
And climbed those rocks that lead up to the baseball diamond

Behind your house, and was gone
Leaving you, the severed red ribbon, and the faint smell of dried roses
Against the cold upriver night, without speaking a word
He told you the truths of your future, the possibilities of love, and the
Consequences of dreams that are never dreamed but are unanswered
Like any old undreamt dream that lay never noticed

The Floating Gardens

Hammertoe and amber gee
This illicit gambled candle of calm drought
Winds upward serpentine yet crystalline
The fallow wrongs of naught

Soothsayers shallow slumber
Woken springs spitting jumble berries
Clothed in rattle down
With toes aplenty jewels for fairies

Gliding along minister loggias
Wrapped in cast steel aster tone
Reaches to touch personal submersibles
Spindling towers five o'clock roan

Vast the slitting sagging cases opened
Tumbled treasures candy doll
Eyes a gander glass trembled frown
Each sequester picking angle scowl

Abdication is sweet succor
Tasseled in silk repose
I swoon forever after flowers
Are swindled midst the rose

THE LETTER "R"

A man walking at *Mauthausen* was so bent over I couldn't figure out
How it all worked, how he walked or dressed or lived
He was bent into the letter R
It was like Kafka inventing a machine that tortuously engraved flesh
With the name of your crime as your horrific final punishment
The *lager* had engraved on him the hateful crimes of others
He was the boy they sculpted with perfect insane beauty
Into a letter that starts repulsion, rape, and rage
Into a crooked old man who walked with a purpose
To redeposit his legacy, his letter-flesh, into a bent
Sunflower for all to see that rose over 500 feet into our brains

Bursting through the wall between living hell and cold cool death
Banging on the door of insanity with the calm reason of murder
Murder so foul it must have a new word to distinguish it from the
Normal murder we so know and love
This new word like the word for G-D of the pious Jews
Known by many names but unspoken all
Names lying about in unopened closets in our minds and in
Dusty hallways with graffiti in blood carrying
Stones so heavy that to haul them up the Stairs of Death they
Built this castle prison of pain in the awesome beauty of the Alps

Planning a prayer service for 141,700 people
Reciting the *Song of David* and playing a partisan fighter song on the flute
A surreal scene unfolded at *Kaddish* prayer with covered
Heads and heavy hearts where tears flowed 70 years later
We stood at Gusen where the slaves had to build a bridge in one day
To carry the train to the tunnels where they would work and work and work
And die
It was a beautiful night
When up from the river under the bridge rose two magnificent horses
One with a tightly braided mane
Ridden by teenaged girls they just couldn't know what they'd come upon

There was more—a soccer rally across a field at a nearby school
With war drums and chants and smoke bombs to mark our Sabbath
But the best was saved for last
I had noticed an older woman across from me in the prayer circle

At once smoking and crying
But once we were done, she was upon me, in my face
The cigarette thrust in my face between her sausage fingers
For the third time in my life I was attacked for being a "dirty Jew"
Once on the playground at grade school, once in a fight with my ex-wife
And now after praying for the unconsecrated dead at *Gusen*

So it is with a heavy heart that I write this
Short poem to remember the bent over man
The "R" man I called him
With his crisp white dress shirt and shiny shoes
He wasn't wearing that prison uniform anymore
But many did, these survivors of the most terrible place
There really aren't words
There are words for the edges of what we might have seen
Or imagined could happen but they fail to penetrate
The inner depths of the process that took a farm boy
From his Mother
And turned him into a human upper case letter
An upside down letter L, an askew letter S

Home on the streets in America
Was that he again? I espied a man with the same bent quality
The same vintage
Those shiny shoes scraping the pavement
But when I caught up with him his face was different
Pocked with life's marks
Creased with life's dealings
I got a cold feeling he wasn't striding with purpose
He wasn't righting a wrong
Yet the mystery of how life turned him into a capital letter
Hung about him like smog
I gave him a wide berth to maneuver down the street
And stopped to wonder at the shape of life and
At the beauty of the pause between the birth blood and the death rattle
For that's all we'll ever know

THE SACRED AND THE PROFANE

Drowning in a milkshake of self-doubt
Swirling, sliding down the sides of a cheap slippery
Paper cup of my own sadness
I grip myself my chest hard at night I hold myself
Against the hours when I find no right position
To sleep and am doomed again to listen to the cars
The drunks right on time their cigarettes under my
Window keeping it cracked for the trains
That whoosh by, the smaller elevated clickety
The larger metro the old northwestern line
Rumble toots powerful over the old overpasses

Taking out the copy of *Tyrannus Nix* by
Ferlinghetti that you gave me I found a long
Red hair with a loose knot tied in it
Then I remembered putting the hair there
One of those magical days we spent together
It came back in a flood the trip to Gusen
The walk behind the houses with the secret
Gardens that spoke no tales of the skeletons
That walked through here did they ever find
An apple on a fence post? From doom to death
They walked now we walk with light fingertips
Touching and our breath drawn against the
Crisp morning air we were inhaling each other

Like that leaf of childhood wonder one side
Soft the other rough I vacillate between the
Scared and my own profanity the Sacred with
External influences very helpful in finding
The profane available from a seemingly
Endless supply of internal and social vitriol
My own sacred is what I crave
Rumbling around I call it
The late night rumble
Where my feet make doughnuts
In the wood floor
Around and around I prance
To remember where things are kept

Where things were left
What things are lost, and which remain
What are sacred, and which profane

THESE DAYS GROWN INTO ADULT NIGHTS/WITH BOOKS

1.

These days grown into adult nights
Are lonely
The kind of lonely that has steam and mist
Built into its picture frame
The city perfect in its glance
A shrug, really, over the shoulder
Sending you off down a street
Not well lit
Where if you lose your keys
You'd be searching in the morning
In the snow

It's perfect the box I made
All jade and perfumed and connected
To every fiber of me that I have
In perfection comes the quiet skip

Cuffs upon wrists
My darling boy they slip them on
We shoot the body down
Into the street
Left in a jangled pose
Near god's creation

A gathering up
Reckoning they used to name it
In the great American backwoods
Of twisted cover your tracks logic
Any man can win the disjointed race

These long nights of sweeping streetcar glory
Of silver finesse the light did catch my eye
I sit wishing I smoked a bit
I'd roll that cigarette in longer browned tips
My fingers hardened by love and harmonica hiding
The open hole I wailed
A whole long while past my stop

2.

With my friend's books one thousand volumes
In my home stacked taller than me
Against the laundry wall
They smell of old days when the sun turned younger

To think these books are worth any money
I could sit in Peekskill and sell them while
The sheriff watched
I'd trade them for squat water glasses from the fifties

Old books to wrap my dreams in
Like old socks sequined where secrets are stored
In any old day I'd be happy humming my song
The riches of my groaning cupboard fanciful indeed

But this crazy loon night
With feet moving to not be frozen in rail bed ponds
I would give it back for a chance to be whole
Sitting in your bed chest all electric plum cherries

Yet the yawning night looms
Infinite in its dark curve of longing
It welcomes me with clipped hours
Of silent running of eyes wide seeing

Tide of night to dawn
An airport breathes and I gather stones
Chits they are paper and rock equal values
Feet first I walk myself home home home.

THE STACKS

(With the song "Downtown" as sung by Petula Clark as an inspiration)

It's all there at the public library
The library of my youthful wanderlust
And now in those very stacks
I find myself leafing through books again
There are young lovers in the corner
I never kissed a girl in the library
But I think it would be a fine place to have a
First kiss when you are 14
No my mission is clearly more middle-aged driven
Finding writers who touch my screen
Filling it up with their words
Finding poets who wrote in Sanskrit, and German, and Hebrew
And all the new books! I wonder how many there are
Published in the past 40 years
Since you used to see me, sitting in the music carrels
Headphones on, listening to Gesualdo and Harry Partch

I used to have a dream
That I would be a dragon, a book-eating one
And I'd start at the back of the stacks
Eating books as I went through
Until I had devoured a whole section
Say, Sports or American Literature
And I could retreat to my parent's home
A very full book-eating dragon
I'd belch out a book or two, like Mark Twain
Or a volume about Jackie Robinson, and how he broke
The color line in baseball
Today I laughed at myself, remembering that dream
I think I wanted to be bigger than all the books
Towering over me in the endless stacks
Knowing that I could never read them all
I could just eat them, and the words would be mine
My dinner, I would remember each one even though I'd never give
     them back
Stingy, don't you think? Such a dream, I'd destroy the perfect
Socialism of libraries, but now I am a fierce protector of books

Today I found three volumes of Paul Celan
Lamenting somewhat that I had to read him
In English, and not the native German
Thinking about the statement that collective
Memory could never wash away the sins of his
Homeland, of Deutschland Über Alles
But I lugged the books home, with a new
Black sweater that I bought downtown
And laid the volumes out next to my reading chair
In the cozy farmhouse I now call my home
Amazed that the editor took the time and care
To give me both the German and the translation
I practiced the cumbersome words that he originally used
Pen on page, and heart on sleeve
Taking the holocaust into his bloodstream and giving out these clear
    words
Words to sear the soul and etch the sky with the terror of his reason

I did a little wandering through the library
Noticing how different people used it
In this vast Republic of ours
A man who looked very disturbed
Was using the free Internet with headphones
Each time I walked past with a new number
From the Dewey Decimal listings, of a poet
I was trying to find, he was watching another
Doors video on Youtube, from the *Strange Days*
Album, like "People Are Strange" or "Touch Me"
Finally he started watching me as I walked past
Watching him, and I blushed or something
Looking away then, I knew that he was safe and
Not a psycho killer, but just a man in a long coat
Using the public Internet to listen to some old music
The place was filled with in-between people
People who looked tired, who were trying to sleep
And kids pretending to write papers or study, who were
Just copying words down into their notebooks to show to their teachers

I had to pinch myself then
Remembering my own sleepy days in the stacks
Knowing that I had used the library to dream

To write silly papers, or just to meet someone
To rest on a day when I didn't have a thing to do
But especially to listen to music
Before it was all free, just on my computer
Waiting for me
Here I had discovered the glass harmonica
A contraption with glasses filled with various amounts of water
That spun through some mechanical apparatus
The player would wet his fingers and lightly touch the rims of the glasses
And approximate music, the notes ethereal to the ear
Mozart and Satie, played on this thing
I though it was real music, but my teachers disagreed
I do remember a big discussion in music class about it
The same class in the art wing where another student and I debated
The merits of Herbie Hancock versus Bill Evans
Then I was staunchly behind Herbie, and the other behind Bill
Today it seems amazing to me that I even had this discussion in my
    High School
And, of course, today I see both points of view clearly
The unending lyricism of Bill, and the hip lines of Herbie, both are
winners in my Sonic mind

I could write a book about it
The dream-like state of the library where everyone seemed to float on ether
The ether-net, where books are still king
And not some grey lines of type on a Kindle
Like when I was on vacation last year in the Virgin Islands
Everyone was older than me, and richer
They all smoked cigarettes still
And each had a Kindle instead of a book on the beach
I was trying to figure out where I fit in
And then it hit me, I was a library child
I liked the way that books smelled, and how they felt
I liked the old books the best, and I used to imagine
Who might have checked them out in the way back past
You know the loved books, and also the ones assigned for class
They've been fingered, and are loose at the seams
And they've been marked up in pencil, words underlined or circled
It used to piss me off that people would write in a book
But then it hit me that they were leaving their mark for me
And that they were actually trying to learn and know and own the book

My dragon dream then coming into sharp focus
If I had somehow had my way, whole sections would be gone
Some young writer would have been denied her Chaucer, or her
    Dickinson, or Poe

Today the library is everything for everyone
A sleeping room, a reading room, a meeting place
Imagine, there's a special place just for teenagers
Where the latest thing is available and the atmosphere is like an
    MTV set
The kids section takes up the whole of the first floor
Except for a little section with comfy chairs and the latest releases
This is now where the homeless men congregate
And pass tobacco and cigarette papers back and forth
Before retreating outside to smoke
I venture into their tight circle to look at the new books
But I don't take them to the checkout line
I'm more of a four-week checker-outer guy
Been burned with that quick turn around too many times
And faced with a fourteen dollar fine, kick myself that I never read the
    new book
About Frank Lloyd Wright, or How to Beat the Stock Market
No, they're still under the seat of my car, floating around down there
Waiting for Spring for me to find them and return them
I wish my library card said "Been a member since 1960"
That would be cool

Oh, the public library
I recommend it for everyone
And today, I am rewarded
Everyone seems to be here
An older couple chattering nervously in the stacks near me
While I look at the collections of the Beat Poets
A young man muttering to himself, and looking at the sex books
They used to hide these from us, but now every library has a section
    for them
A young girl looking at the paintings on display on the second floor
That stance, resting on one leg, then the other
Looking sideways at the artist's work mounted on dividers
The work recreations of masterpieces, but with modern touches
Like Shakespeare in modern dress, with revolvers instead of knives

It's all happening here, I missed it for years
In my basement days, when I was numb and afraid
I only went to the big box booksellers
But now, I'm back
My soul free to soar in the stacks
To refind Harper Lee and discover Lev Raphael
In my old small town library where you once caught my eye

THE WHEEL

The Wheel it was rolling
It was moving fast
Lickety-split
Moved through this town
Real swift like
Either you caught on
Or that wheel was gone

Compounds into
Silver mix stir with your hands
Something nice and sentimental
That wheel grating on the turn
Motion was its only companion
Swept through the screen
Yearly, you might have remembered
Through the glass the radio said

"The way she wore her hair
The way she accented the color of her hair
It was still and bright
It filled the night
But she's not there
'cause no one told me about her
The way people cried"[1]

The way the wheel was moving
It was black and white
Along the tops of the trees it moved
Teetering tearing topping centrally
The wheel keeps it calendar
It tears the town
The clowns left aside, maniacal
Suspenders red in flight

Been fighting it for weeks
But the center collapsed
Leaving the figurine exposed

---

[1] "She's Not There" by Rod Argent (1964), as recorded by the Zombies.

"I won't rush you,
That's not what I'm afraid of"
Barbara Stanwyck says
It was on our first Christmas tree
That's where we first skinned knees
Lots of girls will set their caps for that boy
Though he goes out so seldom

The note asked *"Who are you, what are you doing there?"*
The note pounded in her head for a week
Bernard Hermann was needed
Here's where strings pay the rent
Slashing upwards strings, cellos and chimes
The music of I love you I miss you we're dead
This was when the wheel was slacking
Having a shot, and the drama thick with activity
The leads coiled with information waiting there available

Free Wednesday the human sneer = all men after six
Horns, tenor sax and flute, we've been here before
"Better than any two people in this room"
Funny how a father was declared insane
In the forties there was a newspaper article
Now it is brittle and older and discarded
But I hold on to it like the truth that it was
Mellow now, older still, with yellow roses by request
As if I ever read the press before sending flowers

This Adolf

Although married, this Adolf was childless, the cruel joke of his pious ways
To have so much love to give in one's heart but to have the thread
break, the cupboard Bare, not a soul to pass his Holy Books to, not a
shoe to tie, or the joy of that little hand On a Sunday walk through the
barren streets of his broken *Shtetl*, which is still a world, A whole world
of smashed crockery and of Daisies pushing up through the clay-baked
Dirt, flattened by a thousand push-cart wheels, beaten by the feet of
those walking from Market to home to *Schul*, and to home again.

Being an Uncle wasn't so bad, this Adolf told himself. One could
almost see the Advantage Over being a Father, there would be more to
eat, and nieces and nephews were everywhere running through the
streets when the curtains were being drawn for Candle lighting.
Dragged home, ears first, to be plunged into soapy water and cleaned
For the day of our Lord, day of rest, day of Men's prayer, Day of
Women's ritual bath, Day of child's quiet misery. This Adolf would
walk the perimeter of the town, thinking of the sacrifices of his
Grandfather and his brothers, to help make such a World possible,
where he could actually think such grand thoughts, where next year
would be better than this one.

For this Adolf was raised to be quiet, pliant, reed-like in his ability to
make all happy, to Offend No one, to skim the edges of a life that
really never got off the ground. Oh, yes, Work held its own rewards,
and this Adolf was no stranger to work. His Father's shop Was now his
own, to marvel at that! The reams of fine linen, the everyday cloth that
Made sheets, pillowcases, necessary garments, the occasional flair for a
boy's bar Mitzvah, a wedding, or a tragic Death that needed to be
marked by one's Finest clothes, one's deepest sobs, one's steely gaze,
one's steady hand. All is solved In Prayer, this Adolf thought, with his
head covered, bent in thought, his thoughts Consumed with a drum
that beat, slowly, down the days of his true and pious life.

When the pangs came, and there was less to eat each week, and his
best customers, and Then his only customers, also bent in hunger and
despair, stopped coming into the shop, At first this Adolf prayed a
little Harder. He naturally thought that the Lord was Testing him, and
his large extended family, as had happened before. His Grandfather
had told Him of times like this, when hard work and constant prayer
were of little Use, but of Great comfort. So this Adolf worked, and

prayed, and was an Uncle who brought Comfort and joy to the little ones at his Brother's and Sister's tables, at times to laugh And times to cry, at all times when an Uncle can help by just being there.

But it was unavoidable, the leaving, the going Away into the world, and this Adolf was No different. Like a scene from the American West, with its wagon trails and palefaces And hunting parties, this Adolf went to the West, to the low countries where he had Heard, through a cousin's careful German script, that work and community welcomed The pious Jew, the hardworking man, the thoughtful Uncle would be *so welcome*, please Come with your wife to Join us for this season of fasting. How joyous it will be to have You here, dear Uncle, so how can one resist? After Tears have dried, after Pledges and Oaths of undying devotion were uttered, there was the inevitable moment When the cart was hitched, the strap was lowered, the animals pulled against leather, and the wooden Wheels lurched into the ruts that took this Adolf out of the Diaspora, to the West, for good, for good riddance.

The West was bewildering at first, for this Adolf had never seen so many people at Once, so bustling, so vibrant. One did not really know where to look, for here were People not like the dirt street life he led; colorful silks, and parasols, and men in top hats And organ grinders with their monkeys and begging one-eyed sailors and well-dressed policeman with polished batons and every conceivable smell and taste and experience. It Was too much, really, but this Adolf took it in stride, for he was led by a strong God Who had residence inside Him, who prepared him to be determined for the journey ahead. Everyday Life was keeping your head down, not asking questions but being prepared to Answer them, to keep moving, to find things familiar in a strange new Home. For what started as a comforting thing—of *course*, We would all like to live together! Here we have our World, our shops, our Customs. Here we have our great Synagogues, the *Mikvah* waits for our Women to Wash them clean, to clean away their sins, and To take mine in the process, the Sins of wanting and needing and hoping and dreaming. Comfort can turn to terror, this Adolf now learned.

For the streets so familiar with their pickled smells of brine, the rosewater Washing the gutters, the fried organ meat wafting from every Sunday window, it Was a Whole world, the only known world, a real world between the confusing Clatter of the *goyem*, the clash of too many things on the street at once, the Blizzard of confusion that modern life had become. Streets so comforting now that we Can't leave them, but all the same, better *here* than *there*. So this Adolf now Walked the perimeter each night, to get a little air, to see what can be seen, Which is now very little, just a wire not to cross, just schoolchildren asking For bread to throw to the dirty rabble one more time, just those children being pulled Away by stern Mothers, to communion, to confession, to baptism, to bed.

Stitching on a yellow piece of cloth, it is supposed to be a Star of our David, but it Lacks distinction, sharp corners, any kind of class, *this honors our Lord?* But the True fingers knew the threading, and the stitching, and this Adolf, who was Known, after all, as a seller of fine linens, and was known to have a steady hand, Now applied his skills to sewing these flimsy stars, not so nice, but *nu?* On the coats of Nieces, nephews, neighbors. It was almost like having the shop again, in the Days when this Adolf the boy could dream about joining the Hapsburg Army, or Hebrew school, or siring a son, or opening a grand shop with linens as far as the eye Could see. This stitching was okay, for it took many days and weeks to complete, Everyone in town stopped by. This Adolf was sated, for now, and the clever Tightening of the ropes was hardly felt by the hungry, frightened ones whose eyes Never looked up now, except at Shabbat services, when they were raised as Directed to the heavens above.

Life became slower, mashed out, flatter. Colors receded from view, replaced with Dingy green, brown, gray, black. The occasional flower startled one to see; a red Dress was unknown. This Adolf made his own rut, for he had a survival bell that Rang and rang inside of him. His rut went, not as a route, but as a labyrinth, it Rode up in him and he pledged his own allegiance to My Rut of Life. And this Adolf worked, almost as if in a dream state, a working fool in a fool's paradise, Making hats with cardboard and old upholstery for the men, making toys with discarded anything for His flock of children, genius turning them into giraffes and Other improbable items that kept the nephews glued to this Adolf's side.

Imagine the surprise of being counted one day. A humorous man, a Nebenzahl, Would laugh at the thing, being a *counter*, after all, is to be a Nebenzahl, to Give the count of the Levites and the Cohens to the

High Priest. Isn't that what Nebenzahls *did*, after all? The irony being
that God did not want the Nebenzahls To be included in the count.
So, from King David, with this rather important Job, to help the
Priests, and to count the flock, but to *Not Be Counted?* The deep
Mystery confounded this Adolf, and had since his youth, but now to
be counted, Such a thing is laughable for a man of humor. Which did
not describe this Adolf at all. Humorless was not quite right, but
cautious was spot on. His Outlook tempered by the longing for the
poor order of his past, as opposed to the Desperate chaos of his
present. The streets now clogged with hungry, crazy Crowds pushing
him, he pushing back. The bar lowered, the surge of humanity Closing
in on this Adolf, his world slowly shrinking, tick by tick by tick.

But to be counted was to be collected, one came with the other like a
    salt and
Pepper set. To be counted is to be collected like a dog found after a
    chase,
With a tug and a cuff. To be collected is different than traveling away
From home, from heart, wheels in ruts before trod. This traveling away
More like a deep, dark fall into Hell, a slow but steady fall, a
Free fall during which you flail and at the same blessed time fall dead
Like a rock into a well, your limbs numb, for you've Given In, you've
Said Yes to this death, this fall, if it promises an end, a final, a stop.
And, like everything else that happens to this Adolf, the
Twist twists, and his collection gave him another lease to test his
Prayer to work, to survive, to eke out. Those wooden beds, twenty men
To a shelf, his every night solace from work. His back, stronger than
Most, his mind, still sharpened from thought, his soul full of forget.
To Survive two years of slavery, for that's what it was, to be Strong
Enough to be shipped to the South, to work, that's a *miracle.*
    A penance.
An everlasting monument to the power of the life force, a lesson for
Smart American and Belgian children at their computer screens,
Taking in the Lessons of this Adolf.

For this Adolf went from hell to Hell, from the flame to the fire, and
We never knew, until this hour, how grand his passion was for living,
How his inner flame never died, how he suffered like a Christ
Being in curious crucifixion, with the same wounds and the same
Light, and the same complicated legacy. This Adolf grew in stature
This week as his true sacrifice came into focus. This man, what was He?

To go into the tunnels, or the mines, at Gusen, to dig a twelve-hour day
On stale bread and milky soup, to be beaten both ways, to have a sense of
Humor at night, a breath of air, to be Alive. This **Man** in my family,
This Adolf, our Adolf, My Adolf. How could a man work so
Hard? I shudder, shudder, shudder. The questions come, and I
Throw them back. "Too hard!" "Ask another!" But I must Know,
The strongest man died the Cruelest death, I know.
All around him was horror unknowable horror.
The needle to the heart. The cruel surgery for spite, for malice,
    for twisted
Medicine. To See This. To pass through these names:
Auschwitz, Mauthausen, Gusen.
Is to take a path, the A Train from Hell to Hell to Hell. The Adolf path.
The Strongest Man I've ever heard of, this Adolf, your Adolf,
    My Adolf,
I love you so.

So we pledge, and pledge again. To make some right in your name.

To take a path that others can't, and bury your spirit as it should be
    buried.

To lift the little children into the light, who were so cruelly taken
To the brink of human tolerance for horror, and pitched over the side.

We pledge, and we pledge again. To stand with those who are true and
Rightful and free, whose ashes and bones are Beneath our feet,
Unconsecrated, drifting. To make that right, we must do.

We pledge, and we pledge again. To Adolf, to my dear Adolf.

TONIGHT'S TANKA

Dogs out on the deck
Dealing with the Holocaust
And teenage drinking
That's a lot on one man's mind
On a cool Chicago night

UNION SQUARE

You see I used to live in this town and I thought I owned it
But that's how everyone feels unless they're on a schedule and a bus

My intent was to make lifelong friends and buy notes from tenor
players
I succeeded in both and stole some notes too they do soak into you

The day Bill Evans died I met Freddie the Freeloader in Union
Square
He was inconsolable so we took a cab to hear Johnny Griffin play

He yelled at the cabdriver all the way to *Seventh Avenue South*
The fare creeping higher as we crossed town to the club

Billy Hart playing with the Little Giant in that triangle room with
mirrors
Lots of opera quotes and calls from the bar between songs for Griffin
specials

I was playing flute on the street in the Village that's where I met
Freddie
He liked my Miles and my Oliver Nelson I was making pretty good
money

Freddie famous for suing Miles after being pushed down a flight of
stairs
At Miles' apartment on Riverside Drive the dark prince gave up a half
a million

That summer I met Dexter Gordon and Dewey Redman and Cecil
Taylor
Richard Baratta and I lived on 16th Street he tended bar at the Tin Palace

Union Square Café was *Brownie's* and the park itself a haven for
smash head
The Irish cops in the subterranean station below the old socialist
pundit ground

Reluctant to leave the station at night for baseball bat beatings

Didn't appeal to guys working on the boat fund the bridge release to
   freedom

   One of many nights we lived grander than the epoch we were
      enveloped by
We were privileged to breath belly before the film business, and
   fundraising

      Became our ways to family and pasture and the wisp of dew that is
         time
Wrapped us and placed us in Evanston, and in Tenafly, gardening for
   the dawn

WOODLAND PRAYER

How simple the Lord's complexity
In building everything we saw on the
Woodland trail we walked
The great tree uprooted had a boulder
Stuck in its sinew snarl of branch and root
When the tree fell it took the rock with it
Now like a piece of glacial poetry
This rock hangs in the air wrapped in tree

Stitching it all together that's the big one's
Great accomplishment I think we as
Salient beings see finally in our
Liquid eyes the flaws in
Structure or function or underpinning
But the brute curve of the big story
That's something to ponder
How a tree picks up a rock
Eventually

Every turn of the trail produces a new
Prayer and one minute to think
The old coast still holds a solemn wonder
A patch of yellow across a field and a stone
Fence, to pull off the road and enjoy the view
Capital protected from purchase and decay
Here examine the strength of drainage plans
Realized with fieldstone cut by a master
The water driven down and under
The road always navigable
In any damn weather

WOUNDED WARRIOR

'Tis true
That often "I do"
Means
Put on the cuffs
Imprison me
Jail me up
That's what they want
Lockdown
People they'll willingly
Want this
Comfort in knowing
You're in confinement
Orange jumpsuit
For love
Rules
One can follow

For knowing
The length and width
Of a cage
Defines much love
Oh they flock
To this rock
With bars
A sarcophagus
With long shadows
All knowing
The lock on the heart
That love can provide

Maximum security
Electronically observed
And monitored
Faceless men
Watching each move
An emotional tunnel
Which one can walk in
Limit to behavior
Crush to dreams

In this love
Many many
Can find peace

Barbed wire
Traded for barbed words
Which cut
And bite
Life contained
In a jar
Wrapped in flags
Stuffed with
Gags to the throat
Eyes slit
If looking is a
Problem
That'll do

Body blows
And truncheon strikes
Daily dished out
For your pleasure
Not the pain of
Fetish love
Not the comfort
Of limitations
Vexations of
Movement
Thought and freedom
Daily searches
Cavity looks
Take away certain
Rights
In return
I'll confess

You become
My jailer then
Do you see?
You wear the key ring
With the hundred keys

And my thoughts cease
To wander so
And slack into
Regular known patterns
Despair for logical endings
I trade for the suit
Trade up
For a real good time
Stop thinking altogether

For we settle
Down
Sell the soul
For the couch
A bull's penis
Of brown leather
A German automobile
Each year
The black interior
Defines the true meaning
Of love
Chrome knobs
Wooden hearts
Little key chains
To fence me in

Oh this hardly describes
The eve of your
Birthday
Free again
Although the
Prison
Of the last
Time
Haunts
Still
You can run
The hills are alive
Indeed
And, looking back
See so clear

The hiatus of human
Pain offered to the
Inmates
Of this
Planet

Who willingly
Take the gag
The bit
And settle down
On the couch
"I had a couch moment"
The battle cry
Of freethinking
That freedom
Itself
Came with a heavy price
Rightfully
You remind us
Of this cost
Added up
It's a lot
Quite a bit

So
I'll just wait
The benefit of time
Over space
Over returns
Easily harvested
Wins this race
The walls caved in
Tonight
They craved
In
This nighttime
Onslaught
Of winged flight
For the free man within
My breast
Soared

I learned

Taking the pain
Of my own walls
My own jail
My hell and heaven
I choose
There is a mirror
At the end of my
Old cell
Kept there
In sexy confinement
My old loves
Lined up
Each one a siren
Of memory
And faces I recognize
From torture sessions
I ordered

Never going back to that prison
Stay out of jail free
If I land on that
Square
I've always got this
Card
In my wallet
I can flash it
At the sentry
As they take me down
Again
Wiggle free
And fly away
Strongly sensing
Change can come

Change I can live with
Spend
Or save
Change that allows love
To thrive

A recycled couch
Someone gave us
Red
It was fine
But he hated that
Couch
Traded up
For a better
Jail

That was on your watch
On mine, the couch came
Late
Maybe that's why
The anger, the vilifying
Started to roil
So early
It seems
Steeped in the wars
Of my parent's paradox
I hid my bleeding parts
So long
When flight came
My wings were ready
To stretch out
And take shape

Fight the power
Of love to hate
Of heart to fear
The other inside
Taking stock
Of all that is offered
Today
I chose to run
Away instead
Flight, fear, and fight
Fear
Take away the
Stoolie's power
The *judenrat*

The trusty
That's us
Helping our own
Imprisonment
Matter over mind
Keep your mind
Clean
You'll see the result
Shortly
Of free thought
In a rigid world
You're straight
And they're crooked
You long
Where they
Have shortened things
You colored
Under the rainbow
While they're gray
Pulling down shades
Take the bus
Do dishes
Use the library
Of the mind
Fight the power
Flee the city
Walk that road
Singing still, so clear
So birds gasp
In your wake

AUTHOR'S NOTE: After only recently learning about the atrocities committed at the Gusen concentration camp in Austria, I was stunned to discover that a cousin of mine, Adolf Nebenzahl, was exterminated at this camp in 1945. What follows is his official death certificate from the Austrian government's records.

BM.I REPUBLIK ÖSTERREICH
BUNDESMINISTERIUM FÜR INNERES
SEKTION IV - SERVICE UND KONTROLLE

mauthausen memorial
KZ-Gedenkstätte Mauthausen

Mauthausen Memorial Archives
BM.I. dept. IV/7
P.O. Box 100
Austria - 1014 Vienna

DVR: 0000051

phone: +43-1-53126-3832
fax: +43-1-53126-3386
email: mauthausen-memorial@mail.bm.gv.at
internet: http://www.mauthausen.memorial.at

E-Mail-Adresse:

official in charge: **Dr. Vallant**

file number: **3.500/2354-IV/7/11** (please refer to this file number when answering)

subject: information on the deportation of *Adolf NEBENZAHL* to the Concentration Camp Mauthausen

Dear Mr. Gammer,

in response to your inquiry from August 29th 2011 the Mauthausen Memorial Archives can provide you with the following information concerning Adolf Nebenzahl:

source: Entry registers of the political department (Y/36)

Source: registers of the Postroom (Y/43)

source: Entry registers of the protective custody camp commando (Y/44)

Source: Death registers Gusen (NARA RG 549)

name:	**Nebenzahl**
first name:	**Adolf**
date of birth:	**24.1.** [19]11 [January 24th 1911]
place of birth:	**Szerednye**

BM.I BUNDESMINISTERIUM FÜR INNERES

profession:	**Landwirt** [farmer]
prisoner number:	**69802**
category or reason given for deportation:	**U**.[ngarischer] **Jude** [Jewish Prisoner]*
date of committal to the C.C. Mauthausen:	**8. Juni 1944** [June 8th 1944]
transferred to sub-camp:	**Gusen**
date and place of death:	**25. 1. 1945** in Gusen
given cause of death:	**Kreislaufschwäche;** _____ [blood circulation insufficiency]**

comment: quotations from the original sources are indicated in bold letters.

sources: entry registers (Y/36, Y/43, Y/44); Death registers Gusen (NARA RG 549)

*"**Jude**" ("Jewish Prisoner") Since 1939, persons denominated as "Jews" due to the National-Socialist's race ideology, were deported to the concentration camp Mauthausen. The denomination "Jew" referred to believers of various confessions as well as atheists. As from 1942 the so-called "Endlösung der Judenfrage" ("Final Solution of the Jewish Question") was carried out systematically on German and all occupied territories.

**Please note that the given cause of death does not necessarily correlate with the actual reasons for the prisoner's demise.

The Mauthausen Memorial Archives hope that this information is of any help for you.

September 2011

Für die Bundesministerin (Federal Ministry of the Interior):

Mag. Anita Korp

DEDICATIONS

GUSEN STATION
Dedicated to Martha Gammer

LILY OF THE VALLEY
Dedicated to my daughter, Aria Nebenzahl

LISTENING TO GLENN GOULD
Dedicated to Mark Rubenstein

NINE TANKA POEMS
Dedicated to Jun Fujita

1942 NEBENZAHL REDUX
Dedicated to Miriam Zahler family

PIÑATA OR KRISTALLNACHT
Dedicated to Brian Finley

RAINBOW SHERBET
Dedicated to Fred Simon

THE FLOATING GARDENS
Dedicated to my son, Ian Nebenzahl

UNION SQUARE
Dedicated to Richard Baratta

ACKNOWLEDGMENTS

This collection is dedicated to my partner Karen Finley, who believed in the poems and has inspired my continued attention and devotion to writing, art, and music.

These poems are offered as gifts to my wonderful children, Ian and Aria Nebenzahl; and, in fond memory of my parents, Chico and Irv Nebenzahl whose fighting spirit is an inspiration to me today.

All love to my family around the world, especially the next generation—to Amelia Nebenzahl Ahl; to Zarah, Leyla and Jaydon Zahler; to Violet Overn; to Vince and Marline Johnson; and to Matthew Logan, Clark and Ellie Finley. All love to Will, John, James, Neelu and Brian Finley. Kisses to Myriam Zahler, Solange Goldwasser, Vivianne Akoka, Suzanne Hirschberg, Harold Nebenzal, Rachel Naveh, Michel Zahler, Rick Nemes, Donna Nebenzahl, Stanley Hollander, Bernie and Gail Nebenzahl, Soozie Nichol, Pamela Flagg, Miriam Finer, Candice Bradley, and to all of my extended Nebenzahl and Waggett family.

All awe and grateful thanks to my colleagues involved in Gusen, Austria, in examining our past; hats off to Martha Gammer, Rudi Haunschmied, David Kranzelbinder, Melanie Berger, and especially to my cousin Roby Zahler, who has been deeply committed to our ongoing work in remembrance.

And thanks to Mark Rubenstein, Fred Simon, Bradley Pierce Smith, Al Filreis, Hannes and Herta Priesch, Dona Ann McAdams, Carroll McDowell, Creighton King, Bruce Yonemoto, Mat Gleason, Joel Erenberg, Chris Tanner, John Schultz, Ida and Studs Terkel, Frank Donaldson, Victor Jackson, EG McDaniel, Steve Flugum, Steve Capillo, Ann C. Davis, Nancy Howard Gray, Joseph Zverov, Richard Graef, Jonathon Kozol, John D. Callaway, Joseph Jarman, Sir James Galway, Thaddeus Watson, Joe Kainz, William Russo, Richard Baratta and Jill Cliffer, Joe Killian, Robin Connell, Kenneth Zapp, Bob Testore, Jack Wolfsohn, Jimmie Alford, Corky and Holly Siegel, Andy Somma, Sandy Boyd, Rick Kogan, Forrest Buchtel, Jr., Jim Schwall, Steve Goodman, Mark Rogovin, Homesick James, Big Walter Horton, Eddie Russ, Jeremy Steig, Fred Anderson, Billy Brimfield, Jimmy Forrest, Al Grey, Ali and Mel Torme, Saheb Sarbib, Freddie the Freeloader, and Hank Jones—living and dead the people who befriended me, stood by me, and taught me something about art and life along the way.

ABOUT THE AUTHOR

Paul Nebenzahl is a writer, musician, and painter who lives in Evanston, Illinois, and Sleepy Hollow, New York. As a performing multi-instrumentalist, and composer, Paul has created works for film and television, and has performed extensively in theater, stage, and club settings. In 2012, Paul's poem "Gusen Station" was published in English, Italian and German by the International Committee for Mauthausen and Gusen. His poem "Charles Bukowski" appears in the Silver Birch Press *Bukowski Anthology* (2013) and "Here's to the Singer of Songs" is featured in the Silver Birch Press *Summer Anthology* (2013) and in this collection.